Rave Reviews for Uh, Wow!

"Melody surprised me with her fun, light and playful approach. I really want others to know that Melody can provide a real possibility of a breakthrough."

    - Claire Phillips, Bedford, Tx

"It helped me see the patterns in relationships I've had. Melody presents a very Buddhist way of thinking and interacting."

    - Kathy Staford, Plano, Tx

"In my estimation, the book will be helpful to many...(the) metaphors are appealing, the illustration clear and funny at times, and (the) writing style is such that the ideas of the book are very accessible. I thus trust that the book will be a success. Congratulations!"

    - Ellert Nijenhuis, author **Somataform Dissociation: Phenomena, Measurement and Theorectical Issues and The Haunted Self: Structural Dissociation and the Treatment of Chronic Traumatization**

this changes everything!

MELODY BROOKE, MA

Oh, Wow! This Changes Everything!

©2008 Melody Brooke

Published by Changes Press
1221 Campbell Rd. Suite 271
Richardson, TX 75080

www.ohwowthischangeseverything.com

Edited by Mike Henricks, Marion Dunn-McClure and Hayley Hahn
Cover design by Janet Kent
Interior art and layout by Melody Brooke

All rights reserved. No part of this book may be used or reproduced in any manner whatsoever without the written permission of the Publisher.

Printed in the United States of America
2007 - First Edition

Dedicated to my children and future generations with the hope that they will live in a world of Compassion.

Contents

Acknowledgments - - - - - - - - - - - - *x*

Introduction - - - - - - - - - - - - - - - 1

Chapter 1 The Drama of a Crash Test Dummy   5

Chapter 2 What Drives drama   21

Chapter 3 We Are Confused About Whose Driving   33

Chapter 4 Shifting to a Higher Gear   53

Chapter 5 How we make the shift   75

Chapter 6 The Shift Into Compassion   101

Chapter 7 When Shifting Gears   123

Chapter 8 Living in the New Gear   133

End Notes - - - - - - - - - - - - - - - 146

Acknowledgments

I want to thank everyone who read my first book, **Cycles of the Heart: a way out of the Egocentrism of everyday life**. They tell me how the Cycles of the Heart Model really does change everything. Their stories encourage me to keep working at finding new ways to present these ideas. Additionally I have to thank my husband Mike Henricks whose encouragement and help allowed me to discover new ways to share the Cycles model. His persistent editing and challenging my way of saying things resulted in a powerful and easily understandable book. My dear friend Marion Dunn-McLure assisted in editing and re-writing portions of the book as well. Special thanks go to my daughter Hayley Hahn who made the final edits, finding details that none of the rest of us did. It is also important that I mention a mentor and teacher of mine, Dr. Collin Ross. It was his re-introduction of the drama triangle into my thinking that provided the impetus for me to develop the Cycles of the Heart Model. I thank you all very much.

Introduction

I entered therapy after the death of my fourth child from Sudden Infant Death. Like any caring Rescuer I walked into the counseling office at the College my husband and I both attended, two weeks after my son died and asked about the possibility of his getting some counseling to help with problems I felt he was having. Needless to say, she asked about me and when I told her about my son she insisted that I get some help.

That help eventually got me into a series of groups which were wonderfully supportive and helped me process through a lot of shame and loss from my childhood as well as the recent one. I learned to become "assertive"-which meant allowing myself to vent the anger associated with the loss as well. Part of that process encouraged my anger toward my then husband. Over time I built up a righteous sense of anger toward him for what were clearly inappropriate and oftentimes-emotionally abusive behaviors. Eventually I felt powerful enough to leave him and start a life free of the oppressive stress of living with him. Everyone in the group had done something similar. We all had dissatisfying relationships with our mates and the group leader called them "Perps" or "Narcissists" (even when she had not met them personally). We all left the group assertive - and single.

What the Cycle of Compassion has taught me is that my divorce and the divorces of the other women in the group may not have been necessary. If we had been able to step out of the Victim role and take Ownership of our own dysfunction; if we had been able to have Empathy and Respect for our mates instead of firing anger and shame at them; we may have been empowered to change the quality of that relationship.

This book will help you understand the unconscious patterns of behaviors that keep us stuck in an endless cycle of suffering. But it does not stop there; it also provides a road map for change. Choosing to live an empowered life means facing the blocks to being fully present with our self and others. It means being willing to feel things that have been difficult, if not impossible, to let ourselves feel in the past. It means taking Ownership of the quality of our lives and moving toward a satisfying life.

When I finished my first book I knew that it would only be the beginning. There are so many applications for my model that I expected my second book to be on parenting, or marriage. But as my book has been distributed I realized I needed to write a different kind of book. **Oh, Wow! This changes everything!** is written to empower you to shift into a new way of understanding yourself and others. **Cycles of the Heart** was written as I developed the model and the theories are spelled out clearly and succinctly there. But **Oh, Wow! This changes everything!** takes a different approach, bringing the model closer to home and helping to bring the concepts alive with its stories, exercises and encouragement. It empowers you to take a hold of how our brains run our lives, and the way out of its twisted web. The laws of the mind do not have to rule our lives.

Recently increased awareness of the "law of attraction" has spread around the world. People whom had never heard of the power of our words and minds have now accepted an understanding of the ways our universe responds to our conscious thought. For me, this is an exciting thing. Having been a fan of Napoleon Hills' **Think and Grow Rich** and Norman Vincent Peale's **The Power of Positive Thinking** since adolescence, I am heartened to see so many people taking charge of their lives in new and powerful ways.

What surprises me is that so many of the proponents of the secrets of the "law of attraction" seem to not realize the complexity of the law. Understanding that we need to change how we think is important, and a valuable piece of using the law, but it's not the whole story. If it were that simple the thousands of people practicing the "mind sciences" for the past hundred years or more would all be extremely wealthy. But they are not.

Why is that? If, as **The Power of Positive Thinking** proposes, our thoughts are things, why can't we just change our thoughts and change our lives?

Because we don't always know what is going on in our brain! **Oh, Wow! This changes everything!** empowers you by showing you how your automatic brain reactions impact your every thought and action. Understanding how our brains lie and twist reality, creating fear, anger and shame gives us the choice to react differently. Understanding how to interrupt those old patterns transforms how we think, live and relate to others and ourselves.

So hold on to your seat as you explore the ways in which the shift comes to your door, to the very seat you are sitting in, ready to transform your life!

CHAPTER 1

The Drama of a Crash Test Dummy

Can you hear me?

Have you noticed some people just can't hear what you are saying, no matter how many times you explain it? Probably you have seen the other side, too. Really trying to understan, but their ideas are just so far away from what you can accept that you just couldn't believe they meant what you were hearing. Both of you may be really trying but your reactions and beliefs are so primal that there might as well be a canyon between you.

You may not even feel like yourself, but feel as though you were reading some foreign script. Your reaction to their words directs what you do and say. In that moment, you have a co-starring role as an unwilling Drama Queen.

The Drama somehow explodes into a story you can tell others. You may feel wounded, or even self-righteous. They were, after all, behaving horribly. (Never mind how reactive we were, after all, we wouldn't have behaved that way without their having pushed us to act that way).

You are undoubtedly the type of person who engages their intellect to help you respond to others calmly instead of just reacting. You might even have done a lot of therapy and worked hard on your issues in order to respond maturely to conflicts. You may have learned to be assertive and manage your communications with a degree of savoir-faire. And so it always astonishes you when you leave a conflictual situation feeling hurt, shamed, embarrassed or downright angry.

Survival and the brain

Our brains are programmed by biology and culture to insure our survival in primitive situations. Your brain doesn't really get it that if you perceive your job is being threatened you will not die. It really feels like you will. Your brain doesn't know that if your husband/wife/partner is angry with you and you think they might leave you that you won't die. Your brain doesn't know that when a friend calls your character into question, that you won't die. Your brain doesn't discriminate between actual threat for your survival and emotional threat.

This is because our brains are divided into sections. Our reptilian ancestors brains have three cleanly defined sections: the front part handles smell, the middle vision, and the rear gives us balance and coordination. Those basic survival instincts live between the smell and vision sections so they get to react to inputs first. This primitive part of the brain holds our drives for food, sex and, of course, our "fight-or-flight" response.

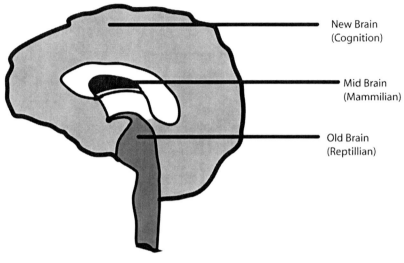

Our Tri-Part Brain

As our mammalian brains developed, more and more circuits were needed to process the increasingly complex life and culture of our mammalian ancestors so our brains grew in size. As we mature into adults, our higher reasoning centers gain more influence over our responses, but we still rely on our "first responder" command post to assist us in our primary need: survival. This relic of the past often reacts before our evolved brains can choose a more appropriate reaction.

It's like you have two brains in one body. Your emotional

states that evolved to help you survive; and the other which is ruled by reason. The fast reacting old brain; and the slower new brain in one package: your skull. Therein lies the drama.

Most of the time you can maintain mastery over your old brain and reason your way out of the extreme dramas of life and death battles. But there are plenty of times when your brain is confused about the level of danger in a particular situation and your brain reacts as though you were fighting for your life. The more we exercise these primitive responses (particularly as a child) the more dominant the responses become. These are the situations when you really want to shoot the other drama queen, but you know you can't. After all, you don't want to spend your life in prison. But, oh, it sure feels right. That's drama. And you, my dear, are the Queen.

The Cycle of Egocentrism

Your brain has developed ways to handle most threats with a reasonable assurance of success. Your primitive brain perceives the threat, and your reasoning brain figures out a way to maneuver through it. The goal is to maintain a sense of power and control over the situation. If you can't to do this, you are likely to die (or at least, you feel like you will). In order to avoid death (or your sense of well being at the very least), you strive to maintain power and control. We have no choice but to survive or die.

When our survival or our well-being is threatened our old brain kicks into gear. But rather than freezing, running away or kicking and hitting our way out of it, our new brain, our higher brain functions, figure out how to respond to the threat. We choose behaviors that are versions of the fight-flight-freeze-submit patterns which are socially acceptable.

These behaviors, applied in what appear to be grown up ways, drive the Cycle of Egocentrism.

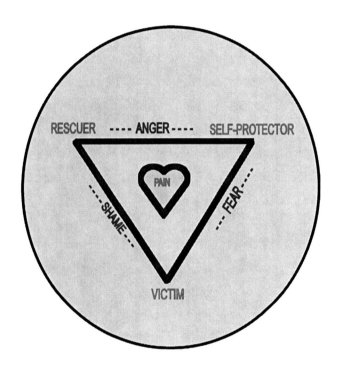

Cycle of Egocentrism

"I am struggling to survive against the world" (the mantra of the Cycle of Egocentrism) then becomes the unconscious core theme of our relationships. Drama Queen's always seek to know "Are you out to hurt me or to help me?"[1] We are so focused on ourselves that what others need or want is relevant only when it furthers our own needs and wants. If you perceive an attacker: you think of them as the Villain and you are the Victim. If we think someone else is attacking another person and we think we can do something about it, we respond as the Rescuer.

Notice there is not a villain in the diagram. When you think you are the Victim, and someone else is to BLAME then you assume a posture that has felt safe before. If a defensive attack and withdrawal has worked in the past then you will likely go into what I call the Self Protector role. If pacifying the other person by trying to fix their problem has brought peace in similar situations, then you will want the Rescuer role. If instead, you feel incapable of deflecting the threat in either of those ways, you can give up your power and become a helpless Victim and gain protection by being too pitiful to attack.

None of this means you are "bad." Drama Queens are not "bad" after all; your survival is a necessary thing! Again, the reality is that you are hard wired to these roles. All of us do all of them unconsciously and automatically; your old brain does not offer any other choices.

We are animals after all. We are wired to survive and our brains automatically release chemical hormones to perceived threat. We feel fear and we respond according to what our experience tells us will help us survive. Our experience is of course a combination of what we have done and what we have seen others do. As children, we watch our parents every move. If our identification is with a mother who is a Self-Protector, then we will most likely take on the characteristics of a Self-Protector. However, if we are more identified with a Rescuer father, we will become more like him. Our parents' model is a schema for responding to perceived threat. All of this happens at an unconscious level, programmed through biology and culture.

The Victim

As the star of your own drama, you are at core, the Victim. Each of us sees our world from our egocentric position. You are the center of your own universe. This is, of course, necessary for your survival and important for procreation. As the Victim you struggle to survive. But you see no way out. You are stuck with the feelings of helplessness, despair, shame, fear and hopelessness. The Victim position is one of intense self-hatred full of guilt, shame and self-criticism. The Victim position is the position of death. In the Victim role, you are so stuck that you cannot take any action to save yourself. You are helpless and dependent and hate yourself for this dependence.

The Victim learns that the only defense is to be so helpless that someone else will take care of you. You must be sure that someone sees your desperate plight. You know you can't do it for yourself so you beg, plead, demand even, that someone take over and do what you cannot. You are desperate to survive and your only hope lies in your ability to attract the attention of some big-hearted person.

As Victims we are too helpless to take any responsibility, still, we know it is all our fault because we are so terrible. At least, that's how we see it.

The Self-Protector

    The role usually labeled the Villain is not, in my opinion, really a bad guy at all. They may be doing things that are dangerous or even hurtful, but the intent is survival. In survival mode you are so focused on your own desperate need to survive that you don't notice other people's pain. It's not that you don't care, it's that your own needs, at this moment, overwhelm everything. You are the Queen of that particular Drama.

    Severe injury, neglect and abuse all make us want to fight back. Sometimes you haven't even framed it as being abused, only that you have been hurt, and therefore have to protect yourself against future harm. I always have an image of a junk yard dog when I think of a pure Self-Protector. But Self-Protectors can be merely shut down, quiet types who retreat from the world by isolating ourselves into work, books, TV, video games or other isolating activities.

The Rescuer

Like the Self Protector, Rescuers need to feel powerful, in control. Care-taking someone else can give a sense of power and control, but underneath, you feel small and ashamed of who you are. We are, of course, all Victims at core and we strive to keep others from seeing how "bad we really are." We do this by being "the good guy." You are the good Queen of your Drama. You protect others from the "badness" you feel by doing "good" things for others. You feel ashamed, defensive and often angry and cover your emotions up with efforts to "be a good person"-because you do not really believe you are, though you want others to see you this way.

We overcome our sense of shame by being the Victim's big-hearted savior. We are as dependent on them as they are on us. We don't act out of Respect, but from a need to feel worthwhile as a human being. We simply don't believe we are really "good enough." Again, we don't consciously think that we are a shameful, bad person, these are unconscious patterns developed during early attempts at survival in our childhood.

Empowerment and Choice

We all have a drama queen in us. It doesn't matter who we are or how mature we are. All of us started as infants and slowly integrated higher thinking into our responses. And all of us get scared or overwhelmed. Certainly it doesn't make any difference how much education we have. But we do have a choice, though it is sometimes very difficult to see what those choices are: our survival instincts confuse us.

I have had the privilege to work with people from all walks of life who have experienced lots of drama and accomplished many things. The people who could fully enjoy their accomplishments were always the ones who could establish and maintain healthy relationships that enabled them to live empowered lives. The media tends to confuse empowerment with outward success.

It's easy to recall the story of Marilyn Monroe. She rose

quickly to become one of the biggest Hollywood stars. She made films with Clark Gable, Dean Martin and Laurence Olivier and won a Golden Globe for Best Actress. So what drove this lively, talented young woman to suicide?

She was married at 16 to James Dougherty in June of 1942, divorced in 1946. Then she met and married retired baseball legend Joe DiMaggio. The marriage lasted 9 months. Marilyn later married playwright Arthur Miller. But Marilyn was unhappy. She consulted with a prominent psychoanalyst. As was common during this time, he prescribed barbiturates and tranquilizers along with psychotherapy. In early 1961, Marilyn and Arthur were divorced. When Marilyn died of a drug overdose in 1962, rumors abounded about her affairs with John and Bobby Kennedy. We can only guess at what occurre or even if she intentionally overdosed, but clearly she had never been able to maintain healthy relationships.

Marilyn lived one dramatic life. I have lost count of the movies made about her dramatic life and death. But who would want to live the life she lived or have had the kind of relationships she had? How empowered do you think she felt?

Life Outside the Drama

One of my best friends used to work for a locally based Telecom company. She had her degree in Computer Science, but since her previous work history was as an elementary school teacher, she was hired in the area of Training. In the time I knew her she was promoted seven times, eventually becoming one of the upper echelon of the management team for her company. During this time she also learned about communication and how to build relationships. She developed outstanding communication and conflict resolution skills. It was her ability to handle relationships at all levels that prompted her employer to reward her with promotion after promotion. She made the choice to manage her work relationships free of the drama.

But the most important relationship we have is with our self. Living outside of the drama starts on the inside. When we spend our lives believing other people are more important or that we are not good enough, we cannot have a positive relationship with ourselves. When we berate ourselves for not doing enough or for being stupid or inadequate we cannot fully succeed in any area of our lives.

After my first divorce a very attractive, successful young architect asked me out to dinner. But since my marriage had ended so badly I believed that no one could love me and that I was not good enough for anyone. I remember my heart racing as he came to the door of my little efficiency apartment. As we ate dinner my hands started to shake and my voice nearly disappeared. Being the sweet man he was, he asked me if being with him was making me nervous. I replied that I had just gotten divorced and that maybe I wasn't quite ready to date. I could barely get the words out I was in a total panic – I couldn't get home fast enough.

What I know now is that I couldn't see myself with this man. He was everything I wanted, but nothing I felt I deserved. The contrast between my self-image and what I imagined in him left me panic-stricken.

Now, I have finally arrived at a place that I can allow someone to love me. I have made the choice for the Victim to no longer dominate my life. Living without that kind of drama has allowed me to let someone love me, and for me to be able to love someone else without reservation. We refuse to see each other as an enemy. That doesn't mean we don't have disagreements or occasional conflicts, it just means that we no longer choose to put ourselves, and each other, in the roles of the Cycle of Egocentrism.

I can't tell you what a relief it is to live with this kind of empowerment. Neither of us seeks to gain power and control over the problems between us; we are able to experience each other with Compassion and joy. You can choose to live differently. You, too, can learn the choices necessary to live an empowered life, free of the drama with which we are so familiar.

Chapter Take Aways

√ We are all Drama Queens.

√ Our old brain dictates our emotions.

√ The Cycle of Egocentrism is our programmed way of reacting to perceived threat.

√ We can make the choice to shift into living outside the drama.

> In the long run, we shape our lives, we shape ourselves. It's a process that never ends, until we die. And the choices we make are ultimately our own responsibility.
>
> - Eleanor Roosevelt

CHAPTER 2

Why we love drama

Drama Queens

Drama is part of being human. We use it to define ourselves and tell the stories of our life. Now, I am like everyone else, I like a good story. But unfortunately what makes a "good story" often makes a really horrible life experience. I have some pretty dramatic stories to tell. They have "good guys," "bad guys" and Victims. Some people feel a life without drama would be boring, but I have learned to fully relish the joy of life without the drama. There are so many experiences that do not need fear or anger to make them fun and interesting. Too often we let our history and the stories on television confuse us into thinking Drama is the only way to have an exciting life.

So the question becomes, can we have an interesting story without drama? Of course you can! Drama is just a plot device to engage an audience, but if we don't care about the characters then we won't care about the drama. Remember "Cheers"? We didn't need bad guys or Victims to keep us watching. We loved all of the characters and wanted to share more of their stories.

Assigning blame won't make our stories more interesting. When our story escapes the simple plot lines of the Cycle of Egocentrism we are free to enjoy our life and the surprising characters that share it with us.

Blame and Drama

Drama starts the moment someone assigns blame. Blame assigns all responsibility for something in order to preserve the illusion that we are, if not perfect, at least not all bad. Or, we blame ourselves and take on all the responsibility for something in order to reinforce the idea that we are worthless.

Blame defines the Victim, Villain and Rescuer roles in the Cycle of Egocentrism.. As a survival mechanism it works very well to quickly categorize the actors in our drama as either friend or foe. But this, of course, is a very primitive way of viewing our world and ourselves. For example: a caveman bumps into a tree, he says "Bad tree, me avoid tree next time me walk this way" or, "Bad tiger eat best friend. Me stay away from tiger."

I am obviously over simplifying here but you get my point. Our brains are wired to assign blame to help identify danger. Unfortunately, the survival part of our brain is so powerful and responds so quickly that it can easily overrule our new, cognitive functions. Why is that?

This is because the primitive mechanism of blame helped us a lot during our formative years. Regrettably, this can lead to pretty severe problems later.

Alexandra* was a beautiful 26-year-old blonde with long sparkling curls that hung around her narrow face like drapery, setting off her pale complexion perfectly. She was smart, independent and competent. She had moved, with little help from her family, from the Northeast to Dallas. By the time I met her she had bought herself a new home in a suburb and was employed making more money than anyone I knew without a college education. But she suffered extreme anxiety and a sense of not being enough. She could not maintain long term romantic or even friendship relationships. Her mother dominated her life with daily calls criticizing Alexandra for how she did everything. Alexandra's father was cold, distant and often overly critical himself. She felt she never measured up to what he expected of her. Her having not finished college was a major disappointment to him and he never let her forget it.

She had learned to blame herself for her parent's lack of emotional support and nurturing. This helped her survive a childhood of extreme neglect. When her parents divorced (Alexandra was only four), her mother retained custody. Unlike many single mothers, her mother was unable to make Alexandra and her older sister a priority. Her mother spent most of her time drinking, smoking marijuana and dating -activities Alexandra's older sister of 14 participated in as well. Alexandra was left to her own wits. She doesn't recall what took place during the two years she was on her own, but her father recalls having found her wandering the streets of New Jersey at six and regained custody of her at that time. Briefly, Alexandra experienced a warm loving environment. Her new stepmother was attentive and nurturing, that is until she became pregnant with her own child. From the time the new baby arrived Alexandra became an afterthought. Alexandra tried everything she could think of to regain her stepmothers' former attention; the only thing that worked was acting out. This way her stepmother interacted with her, and at least noticed she existed.

The only explanation for her parents' neglect and abuse was that she must have been a terrible child. She could not, as a child, see her parents as to blame for their actions. Naturally, her parents would love and care for a good child. So she tried to change the only thing she could change, herself. She tried many different things (including acting badly) to get what she needed. While the acting out sometimes won her the attention she craved, it also reinforced that being herself was never enough. Of course, this heavily reinforced survival mechanism carried into her adult life, partly because believing anything else would destroy her important belief that her parents were good. She knew the problem was her!

When Alexandra learned to recognize that her parents had failed her, not the other way around, she began to let go of blaming herself. Just as important, she didn't trap herself by blaming her parents either. She did let herself grieve the loss of her belief that her parents weren't perfect. Eventually she was able to ask questions about her parents' childhood. She developed an understanding of why they behaved as they did. She developed Empathy for both herself and her parents, while not owning the blame for how they parented her. No longer did she have to believe she was bad in order to understand her childhood. This led to her finding a mate and marrying shortly after ending therapy. She is now pregnant and excited about being the kind of mother she once dreamed of having.

Blame incites the kind of drama that besets us with fear, shame and anger. Discovering an alternate way of thinking about ourselves and responding to others frees us from the false beliefs our young brain used to explain the world around us.

How do we make meaning?

Before coming to therapy Alexandra had a story about herself. A story that helped her make meaning of her world and her circumstances. Our stories help us make meaning of what we have experienced. Human beings are meaning making creatures. We are driven to make meaning out of our lives and our environment. Again, this is part of our survival mechanism. When we can understand what occurred in the past in a logical sequential fashion, we can make conclusions based on what has occurred. We can learn from our past and increase our chances of survival.

These stories move us forward and put endings around certain chapters of our lives. When we have a clear-cut answer in our own minds about who is to blame for something then we can move on. Have you ever watched part of a movie and you never found out how it ended? Your brain keeps going back to the story trying to figure out who was to blame for the drama so that you can come to a conclusion and move on. The same thing happens when we don't understand the drama in our own life. Until we decide who was to blame our minds are driven to keep going back until we finally know where to point our finger.

Making meaning by assigning blame helps us learn from the circumstances and to know how to act the next time. It also helps us recognize danger. Blame has an important personal and social role in understanding our personal and political histories. The all or nothing nature of blame lets us protect our cherished world view by assigning faults wherever it is least threatening. Too often we find it is safer to place all of the blame on ourselves rather than let events challenge our critical distortions.

The first man I married turned out to be what I called a "rageaholic." He was physically large and verbally loud. During the first year we were together he ranted and raved and stormed all through the house. I tried to please him every way I could think of, but nothing helped, in fact, it only seemed to make things worse. I thought of him as being "mean" and "rageful," even "abusive" -though he never struck me. Throughout that time I read articles about the abused wife syndrome and I could see that I was becoming intimidated like those women. I found myself growing more and more depressed.

Eventually I turned to therapy, knowing something was wrong and hoping that therapy could make sense of what was going on. In therapy, they taught me that my depression was anger turned inward. My anger was going in on myself and making me depressed, so I needed to learn how to express it outwardly. They gave me a padded bat and encouraged me to hit the arm of a couch with it. This was very difficult for me to do since it required my owning that I felt angry and somehow that just didn't fit my view of myself. Eventually I was able to allow my anger and did use the bat to hit the arm of that couch. It felt painful at first and I burst into tears. Accepting that I was angry meant I couldn't see the world the same way. Over time I was able to channel my anger into that bat and onto that couch. After that I held my own with my husband, I could stand toe to toe with him and give as good as I got. That resulted in angry, yelling, screaming fights that never had a resolution.

One winter morning I recall standing at my front door as he was getting in his car to go to work and screaming out "F------ YOU!" at the top of my lungs. It just so happened that it had snowed that morning and there was a layer of snow covering the neighborhood. My voice echoed up and down the street.

I recall another fight when we were standing in the living room of our rented house and he was so angry his face was growing redder and redder. He balled his hands up into a fist and BAM! He put his fist right through the wall. Fortunately it wasn't my face and his hand was not injured so we both came out unscathed.

But I was growing tired of his tirades and once our daughter was born I realized I could not let my child grow up in this kind of environment. I was so incredibly angry with him that I would have dreams of hacking him up with a hatchet. Rather than kill him, I divorced him, convinced that he was a verbally abusive jerk of whom I was well rid.

I was convinced that the difficulties we had were entirely his fault. He was to blame, not me. Somehow or another I managed to play such a good Victim that I even convinced him that he was entirely to blame. He once told me that if he couldn't make it with me then he probably couldn't make it with anyone because he thought I had no culpability in our problems.

Now that I am on my third marriage (having discovered my error in thinking I had no intimacy issues) I realize that I did have problems having Empathy for someone else, that I did have trouble owning my part in conflicts, and that I often had very little Respect for my partner. Blaming him helped me keep the illusion that I had no intimacy problems, and that all the problems lay with him.

> I don't believe in devils. Indifference and misunderstandings can create evil situations. Most of the time, people who appear to be evil are really Victims of evil deeds.
>
> - Max von Sydow

Survival and drama

Drama helps us manage the chaos of our lives and create a kind of order out of our experiences. It gives us a hero, a villain and a Victim. It helps us survive by helping us know our place and what we should do. When we have set roles we don't have to question what we are doing, we have an identity that we can use to keep our place in our family and in our world. When someone has wronged us we can take recourse. We imprison the wrongdoers and the Victims get aid and support. We are justified in certain behaviors when we can convince someone that the other person is to blame for our actions. Our behaviors become understandable and justifiable no matter how atrocious if we have someone else to blame for them. Obviously this has good survival implications. Likewise, when we can blame someone else for their behavior, no matter how we have provoked them we are let off the hook, we have no responsibility for their reaction to our behaviors.

    A friend of mine tells the story of a man he was good friends with, named Richard*. Richard and his wife, Anna* were engaged in a highly conflictual relationship. They fought all the time (sounds a lot like my ex-husband and me!). According to the story, she knew what buttons to push when he got angry to push him further and further into his rage. One afternoon he came in and she was in a mood. Anna was unhappy with how he had behaved the night before at a friend's home. She felt he had been flirting with their neighbor by teasing and laughing with this other woman. The minute he got in the door she started yelling at him, she threw a dish towel in his face and told him he was a rotten husband. Richard immediately went into Self-Protect mode and grabbed her arm. Anna started screaming that he was abusing her and that if he didn't stop the police would come and arrest him. He threw her on the couch and tried to walk out. Anna stood between him and the door and started beating his chest with her fists. Richard was a tall, hulk of a man, and he could easily dominate her physically. But he was not yet willing to fight back even though she continued to hurt him. He took her hands in his as she continued to fight him. He felt his rage rising, barely able to control it he threw her toward the kitchen. Anna landed hard on the table and sent it crashing to the ground. Now she was infuriated even further, in her mind he had broken something she liked, a table she had picked out along with the centerpiece. Richard sat on the couch trying to regain control when she walked over to the entertainment center where his prized possession, his CD player, DVD player, speakers and CD's were held. She reached into the cabinet and started throwing the components down onto the tile floor. At this point Richard could no longer contain his rage. He grabbed her hands and that is the last thing he remembered before being arrested for murder. Richard was found guilty of strangling his wife to death with his bare hands. He is still in prison.

You might wonder why I put this story of a murder in a section on survival. There are different types of survival. One type of survival is physical: the other is mental. Richard could survive Anna's assault on his body, but somehow her destroying something important to his sense of well-being was too much. Stopping Anna's attack was all that was possible at that moment, and the fact that stopping it meant killing her was irrelevant.

When our brain is in survival mode the Drama escalates out of control. We are cast into a role in the Cycle of Egocentrism and we have no choice but to battle for survival. The interesting question here is: Was Anna a Victim or a villain?

> Throughout my life I have always been amazed that people couldn't listen to other people, that they couldn't hear their best intent that there seemed to be an enormous need to demonize.
>
> – Warren Farrell

Chapter Take Aways

√ Drama is an accepted part of being a human being.

√ The assignment of blame initiates the Drama.

√ The survival part of our brain is so powerful that it can easily overrule our new, cognitive functions.

√ With blame we absolve others whom we feel more comfortable absolving than blaming, allowing us to hold to our fantasies.

√ We can blame and feel free of responsibility for what has occurred letting go of any sense of shame or guilt.

√ Drama gives us a hero, a villain and Victim.

√ Our behaviors become understandable and justifiable no matter how atrocious if we have someone else to blame for them.

CHAPTER 3

We Are Confused About Who We Are

What are we anyway?

For some reason we humans tend to think we are our thoughts and feelings. We think those worries and moment-by-moment streams of thought are the essence of who we are. We think those thoughts represent our self. But who is listening to those thoughts? Who is feeling those feelings? Some other thing, some other idea of a Self has to be the one listening to the thoughts and experiencing the feelings. I know it's a radical idea but we are not the thoughts and feelings that we have. We are something else, something bigger, beyond those thoughts. We are the Self that is listening to those thoughts and feeling those feelings.

You see our bodies are where we live. Our bodies are information-gathering computers, so to speak (I say this loosely because our human computer is so much more complex than any electronic device ever designed that it's not a fair metaphor). Our bodies are designed to gather information and deliver it to our Self. Thoughts represent the information, but they are not the Self. To say that we are those thoughts would be like saying that the data on a computer is the computer. We are something separate from those thoughts and feelings. We are the experiencer, the recipient of the thoughts and feelings, not the thoughts and feelings themselves.

So, for example, if I say "I am so stupid." This is a thought. It has no validity other than that it is a thought. But typically, if we have this thought we think that it's true just because we thought it. Our thoughts are just thoughts. They have no reality in and of themselves, but they do of course, have a huge impact on how we feel and experience our life.

Now comes the really interesting part. Remember our primitive "first responder" brain? It communicates with our body using hormones and with our mind using simple, pre-formed thoughts. "Watch out! There! He's bad!" The limited thought vocabulary of our primitive brain can only pass on its quick recommendation using broad strokes of black and white.

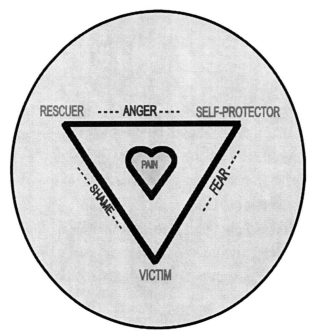

The Cycle of Egocentrism

We are hard-wired to quickly identify who or what is to blame. Identifying who is to blame helps us know how to react in a dangerous situation and determines our next course of action.

The moment we figure out who to blame, either ourselves or someone else, the cycle begins. Blame assigns all responsibility for something so we can quickly decide what to do about it. This works great when a split second decision is needed to get through an immediate crisis. Most of the time, our decisions don't need to be made that quickly. But we have already cast the players into their roles and we are hesitant to second guess our decision (really it was a primitive reaction). In our split second blame game, we either absolve ourselves of responsibility to preserve our illusion that we are perfect, or we assume all responsibility to reinforce our worthlessness.

These pre-programmed thoughts and feelings define the roles of the Cycle of Egocentrism. All three of these pre-programmed sets of thoughts are our automatic reaction to the perception that we are being threatened, real or not. Understanding how these automatic thoughts can dictate our choices is key to breaking free from the trap of Egocentrism and into the Cycle of Compassion. Since we are not our thoughts and feelings, we can take in the information that the thoughts and feelings provide us and then choose how we want to respond to them.

All three of these sets of thoughts and feelings are a part of us. While we may have one that we tend to slip into more than another, they are all part of our way of relating to the world. As you read these descriptions, realize that they all apply to all of us in different situations. Often we even switch back and forth between different strategies while in the midst of a particular circumstance.

The Victim

A true Victim does not contribute to whatever caused their suffering and is powerless to stop it. These are random acts where there is a huge power differential between the Victim and the perpetrator. Think earthquakes or people who abuse their power and authority. When someone assumes the Victim role in the Cycle of

Egocentrism, they believe everyone is more powerful than they are and that bad things happen to them not because they do bad things, but because they are bad.

In the Victim role, we live with hopeless despair. We can't change on our own and we are undeserving of rescue, though we desperately hope that someone more powerful will take pity on us and solve all of our problems. We don't deserve it, but we want it. This is a reasonable survival strategy when we believe we are powerless and that there is no other way out of our situation. Passive hopelessness and despair keep us stuck in the trap. At their lowest, Victims even look to death to rescue them.

The Victim develops a habitual way of relating to the world with helplessness, hopelessness, shame and no accountability. This way of life is self destructive, potentially violent and a certain sentence to a life of misery.

The Victim position drives the Cycle of Egocentrism. In the Victim position, we take no Ownership of our actions or feelings. We honestly believe that everyone in the world is "doing it to us." We desperately seek someone or something to blame for what does not work in our lives. We try to manipulate others into attempting our rescue, (because we honestly believe that we can't do it ourselves). Of course these rescue attempts fail, but it provides more people to blame for our plight. They could have saved us if they wanted to! After all, the Victim sees their Rescuer as one more person with more power than they have and themselves as horrible, shameful and pitiful Victims.

The Victim's paradox is being both be the center of the universe and worthless at the same time. In the Victim role, we have no sense that we exist separately from the world around us. When we are unhappy, it is because nothing in the world is happy. We are not separate from our mothers' unhappiness, or our brothers', or our own-it's all the same. There is no self that is separate from others.

As the Victim, we blame everyone else for our situation, and literally cannot see how we could do anything differently. The moment anyone suggests that we could have some responsibility for our situation, we are driven further into despair by opening the door for the immense shame we hold within. The shame reinforces our powerlessness and anyone who suggests we could be different becomes a perpetrator in our eyes. We are so pitiful that they have no choice but to try to build ourselves back up by telling ourselves "it's not your fault."

The Victims' View of Themselves and the World

Victim's, like the other roles in the Cycle, are consumed with their perceived mistreatment. All of them are angry, self-righteous, controlling, power-hungry and, ultimately, in tremendous pain. Admitting their part in their current mishap would suggest they had power when they want desperately to believe they have none. The paralyzing contradiction in the Cycle of Egocentrism is the crushing need to deny our role while still believing we are to blame for everything. The black or white world of our primitive responses tells us if we are just a little bit at fault, then it is all our fault. This is entirely too much to bear.

While the other roles in the Cycle take action to minimize their pain, the Victim simply gives up. The typical Victim script sounds like this: "I am terrible at (whatever job we were trying to do)," "I shouldn't say anything else," "I have no right to try to do anything," "I am so bad," "I am so stupid," "Why did I even try, I should know better, I am such a failure."

Blame

As the Victim we accept all blame for whatever is occurring, but we avoid any sense of responsibility. How do we do that? Well, we say 'It's all my fault." We are not capable of doing anything differently; we are just "bad" or "stupid." This means if we are to survive we must depend on someone more capable to do things for us. We appeal to the Rescuer to take care of the situation. We beg, we plead that we can't do it and, of course, we don't really deserve the help, but can't you just take mercy on us?

But these self-blaming thoughts and feelings can take on huge proportions and destroy our sense of value and our place in the world. We don't realize this is what is happening. We think these thoughts are true. That makes the thoughts dangerous to us and to our relationships. We think we are so stupid, bad and despicable, (whatever names we call ourselves) that we should just die. We think so badly of ourselves that we allow others, and ourselves, to abuse us. We ignore our needs, we are not careful with our bodies or our things. The world begins to reflect back to us that we are as bad as we think we are and that we are as to blame as our brains think. The Victim position is the position of death.

Lorraine's story

Lorraine* was a client that I inherited from a series of other counselors who had, in Lorraine's words, "Dumped" her. At 45 she was separated and had two teen-aged children who were living in Hawaii with their father. According to her, they went to live with him because he was more financially stable than she. This man had never divorced her (in spite of being seriously involved with someone else) because he knew she needed to have his insurance, additionally he occasionally gave her air fare to come visit her children and supplied her with emergency financing when she was desperately in need. Lorraine's childhood had been horrid. Her parents were dictators, who forced her to care for all her five younger siblings, keep the house spotless and need nothing from them. Additionally they neglected her when she was ill, causing her permanent disabilities and subjected her to sexual abuse and even prostitution. My heart went out to her; she had raised all 5 of her siblings to be successful adults without any help. One was a doctor, another a lawyer. She herself had, for a long while, been a Respected junior architect but she had recently been laid off due to her own inability to function at work. The problem was that she had become so entrenched in the Victim role that she was constantly flirting with suicide. She had made numerous attempts over the years, some quite serious.

Then her health began to fail. She reached out to her family for help, but they had never acknowledged physical problems as having validity and this was no different. They helped her some financially at the beginning but when she failed to help herself in any way, they quit. At 48 she had lost her credit, her health and was on the verge of losing her home. She really believed that her badness was the reason all the awful things happened to her. She saw suicide as her only way out. She refused any other options for treatment, for housing, and no job was right for her. Hopelessness and despair radiated from her. Even educating her about how her brain tricked her into thinking that self-blame made sense was not enough.

Eventually she attempted suicide again. This time she landed in a hospital where she was given an addictions counselor and something about this model clicked for her. She suddenly saw the Cycle of Egocentrism's addictive process and how she had gotten hooked into the cycle with thoughts of suicide. She realized she was trying to escape the pain and hopelessness with the idea of suicide. She was using the idea of suicide to medicate her fear of being stuck in the misery.

Gradually she was able to take incremental steps toward changing her life. The last time I heard from her she had sold her home and moved to a small group home in Hawaii to be close to her children. Her health was improving in the warm climate and she had stopped using suicidal ideation addictively.

How being a Victim helps us survive: not thrive

Survival is imperative. But in the Victim role that is all that we achieve. It is not a happy, fulfilled life. It is a life of pain, drama, conflict and despair. There is no way to thrive from the Victim role. As the Victim we cannot take action for ourselves so even the appearance of thriving cannot be allowed to continue. We are dependent on others and are stuck without any hope of becoming more than a shameful pile of nothing. This is the lie we told ourselves in order to survive the threats we dealt with growing up. These threats did not have to be assaults on our bodies; emotional threats create the same result. We had to blame ourselves to preserve the goodness of the people we depended on for survival. We don't have to just survive now. Now we can choose to thrive.

Self-Protector

Protecting our self against any perceived threat is a basic instinct of survival. The Self protector's position comes about when we perceive ourselves to be under attack or at threat of attack at all times (our world does not feel safe). In order to survive, we instinctively feel we have to keep on guard.

According to the Drama Triangle, as it was originally in Stephen Karpman's[1] scheme, there are the three positions: the Victim, the Rescuer and the Perpetrator. This is the traditional and theatrical version of the triangle. According to Webster's dictionary, to be perpetrator means to "bring about or carry out (a crime or deception)." In this position we may hurt other people, but our only interest is self-protection. A more appropriate name for the "Perpetrator" position is Self-Protector.

As a Self-Protector, we are at core, a Victim. We do not think of our self as a Perpetrator at all. In fact, we would feel offended if someone were to suggest such a thing. We are trying to reduce the pain in the world (ours), not add to it! In the Self-Protector position we see ourselves as the protagonist in the drama of our life.

Self-Protectors are motivated entirely by a desire to avoid pain and fear. We honestly feel we are in a weakened position, but we are determined not to be seen as weak or helpless. Our desperate, self-absorbed attempts to protect ourselves from pain, fear, shame and helplessness are seen as perpetrative by others.

It is from this position of desperation that we may attempt to control others through intimidation and terrorism-or avoidance-and may possibly resort to brute force. We are so desperate to control our sense of helplessness that we will do, at times, almost anything to get control of the situation at hand. We are scared to death, feel weak and powerless (which is terrifying) and we must, through whatever means we can, regain a sense of power and control. Anything less feels as if we will die. We cannot cope with feeling out of control, fearful and weak.

The Self Protectors' View of Themselves and the World

The Self-Protector needs power and control to fend off the oppressive pain of Victimhood. An emotionally healthy person sees the world with a full color palette. Their self esteem does not demand perfection to know they are decent and worthy. But as Self-Protectors our black and white world constantly tears at our self–esteem. We can never be perfect enough, so our worth comes from whatever power and control we can achieve. This false sense of self-esteem is fragile and requires continual shoring up[2].

Self-Protectors keep the world at an emotionally safe distance. We stay too long at work, drink too much, avoid eye contact, and fill our time with busyness. When we adopt the Self-Protector role, our desperate attempts to keep others from hurting us can appear aggressive and just plain mean. Wallowing in our own fear and pain, we are unable to see the impact we have on others.

My step-dad was a supreme Self-Protector. His father was an alcoholic who died of sclerosis of the liver, and his mother was emotionally distant herself, demanding perfection from him in everything he did. He married my mother at 20 and took on an instant family. Working so hard to support us fit right in with his Self-Protector role. It allowed him to remain emotionally distant from us, and my mother, as they struggled to make our little family work. My Dad was never abusive, but he was never physically affectionate or verbally engaging with any of us kids. He tried, in some ways, to connect, but it was always in circumstances in which he had complete control. By finding jobs for us to do for him, he was able to interact with us, but at a distance. For some Self-Protectors, our need to feel power and control reaches dramatic proportions

At our worst, as Self-Protectors, our sense of alienation from reality can be enormous. We sometimes behave in inhumane, abhorrent ways in order to gain that sense of power over our immediate surroundings.

Blame

In the Self-Protector role, we are at core Victims, so we are stuck in blaming. When we feel afraid, we look to see who or what is threatening us. Our needs are not being met and we fear that the other person is not or will not take care of our needs. We get angry and adamantly express our frustration at the other person for having withheld from us what we clearly need. How we react to that anger depends on which response makes us feel most in control. For some it is intimidating the other person through yelling, hitting, or grabbing. Other times we might choose withdrawal and emotional numbing. Either way, we are blaming the other person for deliberately withholding from us and for being incapable of responding to our needs without our efforts at manipulation or direct control.

Lawrence's Story

Lawrence* was a master Self-Protector. Several years after his divorce, he married, Nancy*, a woman 20 years younger than he. For the entirety of their marriage he was the king of the roost. He would bellow at her from one end of the house for her to come do his bidding. He dictated how money was spent and when, and how Nancy dressed. If she did not comply with any of his commands he punished her in varying ways, including giving her the "silent treatment" and denying her the things she wanted or needed. Nancy was unable to have children of her own, so many years into the marriage she and Lawrence began taking in foster children. The children they brought in were all teenaged girls. Those who observed Lawrence and the girls together suspected that he was sexually abusing them, but it was only reported many years later once the girls were grown. Lawrence and Nancy continued to live together even after the abuse was reported, and they went into therapy together. During therapy it came out that Lawrence had been physically and sexually abused by his father, and that he had left his first family because he had feared he would not be able to control his own impulses to do the same to his children. Nancy, in spite of her family's horror, remained married to Lawrence. She had Empathy for what he had been through and forgave him for his Self-Protective way of adapting to his world. Lawrence continued to live with depression and struggled to remain functional after the abuse was disclosed. Eventually he shot himself in the head with a pistol.

How Being a Self-Protector Helps Us Survive: Not Thrive

Obviously, Lawrence did not thrive. Like most people who are so terribly caught up in the Cycle, he adopted his way of coping as a child. He opted to become like his abuser. Most do not replicate their abuser as closely as Lawrence. In order to avoid further persecution themselves, they become like their perpetrator. It is a strategy that works in extreme circumstances. It can also work in less extreme circumstance to help a person feel stronger and less likely to be hurt. Body-builders often build up physical strength to help themselves feel capable of protecting themselves against those who have or could hurt them. Self-protection is like that. We find ways to shore ourselves up to appear intimidating and keep others at a safe distance. Sometimes we maintain separation by withdrawing behind a silent wall that prevents people from getting close enough to hurt us. Other times we do it by being loud, bossy and controlling. But however we do it, it is only a method for survival, not for thriving. Our pain remains hidden behind our protective barriers and no one really knows the wounded vulnerable parts of us. Because of the Self-Protector's nature, we often hurt the people closest to us, hurting ourselves in the process.

Rescuer

The Rescuer role is generally seen as the opposite of the Self-Protector. Rescuers appear to have some power or control in the Victim's situation. As the Rescuer our role is to support the Victims' weakness. We repel the harm and difficulties directed toward the Victim. We believe ourselves to be motivated by Compassion and caring.

In the Rescuer role we are also, at our core: a Victim. Through the role of Rescuer, we gain enough of a sense of control and power to allow ourselves to tolerate being alive. Without appearing to be, we are protecting ourselves from the shame of being a Victim. Through rescuing, we gain an improved self-esteem and a sense of having some control.

As Rescuers, control is the key to our surviving in the Cycle of Egocentrism. We are struggling to maintain an image of ourselves as Compassionate, generous, altruistic, noble, philanthropic and chivalrous. Underneath we are consumed with a feeling of shame that no amount of giving and rescuing can appease. A righteous sense of anger toward the "oppressors" or "perpetrators" of those we attempt to rescue is what drives us.

In some cases, through acting in the Rescuer role, we actually seek to keep the Victim indebted to us. The end result remains the same... the Victim stays weak and dependent. Then, as the Rescuer, we remain chained to the Victim, held captive through our own success at rescuing. And as for the Victim, they are robbed of opportunity to grow and strengthen from the challenges that confront them.

The Rescuers View of Themselves and the World

The only time we Rescuers feel good about ourselves is when we are fixing someone else's problem. Focusing attention outside spares us from the internal pain, helplessness, and despair of being at heart, a Victim. Just like the Self-Protector, we want control, but as Rescuers we seek control by protecting others from knowing how badly we feel about ourselves. Also like Self-Protectors, we are unaware of the impact our intrusive and disRespectful behavior has on others.

As Rescuers, the more chaotic our world becomes, the more controlling we become. To manage shame, we work hard at "impression management." We believe we can control other's perceptions of us and our families. We believe we can control what our children perceive, what they feel, and how they will "turn out." There is very little that we believe we cannot control.

We Rescuers get our sense of value by being in charge and controlling everything. While we do not think of what we are doing as controlling, the people around us do. We are lifted out of our shame by being very important to others. Without the ability to do for others, we don't exist. Our self-esteem is nearly non-existent, we shore up our false sense of worth through doing for others.[3]

We believe on a core level that it's our job, as Rescuers, to save the less able, or less fortunate, of the world.

Blame

Like all participants in the Cycle of Egocentrism, Rescuers are Victims. We believe others in the Cycle Victimized us, denied us the space to be ourselves, and forced us into the role as our only hope of survival. We also believe we are bad and we deserve it. We blame ourselves for being Victimized, and for not stopping terrible things from happening to others and ourselves. We learned as children, we could avoid being damned, criticized and sometimes even abused, by taking care of others. As a helpless child we found that we could get approval, love, affection and even favors by doing things to help others. So we are taught by repetition over a lifetime that the way to get our needs met is to care take others. We also found that doing for others makes us feel better about ourselves. We need Victims to take care of whether they really need us or not. They lift us out of the shame that comes from our core belief that we are to blame for everything unpleasant.

Roxanne's Story

From the time Roxanne was seven years old, she took care of her younger siblings. She recalls going in to the baby's room to feed her youngest sibling while her mother slept. She did whatever she could think of to help her mother care for her five younger siblings, including entertaining them and finding activities for them to keep her mother from having to deal with them. When she married, she too wanted lots of children; she had four of her own. Her husband became an angry drunk and began hitting her when he was unhappy. When she finally had enough she was pregnant with her fourth child and went to her mother for help. Within days her mother told her she had to find someplace else to live. Roxanne, being the Rescuing trooper that she was, did not question this and ended up living in tents at a camping site, telling her kids it was an "adventure." Eventually she got through school and began teaching, working as an advocate for children. It didn't take long before Roxanne fell apart. She had lived her whole life taking care of everyone else and ignoring her own needs. She became severely depressed and suicidal. Starting therapy she began to recognize the patterns that ruled her life. Roxanne began to see that her rescuing behavior was keeping her children stuck in something psychologist's call "learned helplessness." This "learned helplessness" is taught when a child has everything done for them and the child learns he is incapable of doing things for himself. She did not want to do the same thing to her children, but when she tried changing these behaviors she would be overwhelmed with shame, feeling that she was being a "bad mother" by not care taking them. Eventually, she was able to develop Respect for her children and let go of the Rescuing behaviors. It wasn't easy for her children, now teenagers, to accept and they fought back becoming angry and resentful, at first. But over time they became competent and responsible kids. This forced Roxanne to face the shame that she had been carrying since childhood for the abuse by her father. She had secretly been sexually abused by her father and had been avoiding those feelings by Rescuing anyone and everyone. It hasn't been an easy path for Roxanne, but she is now well on the way to Respecting herself and her children.

How being a Rescuer helps us Survive: Not Thrive

Rescuing gives us control over feeling like a Victim. As children, and even as adults, we cannot tolerate the helpless, hopeless despair and shame of being in the Victim position. Rescuing allows us to feel good about ourselves, in spite of our belief in our badness. We can pretend that we are "good" when we believe that we are "bad." It works to give us a sense of power and control. But in that process we lose ourselves. We lose connection to what we want and need. We also cannot let others help us, because we would feel too ashamed. We can never experience true intimacy and reciprocity in a relationship because we can never let someone really see us. We don't want anyone close enough to see how "bad" we think ourselves to be.

Chapter Take Aways

- √ Remember we THINK we are something different than what we ARE.

- √ BLAME sets the Cycle of Egocentrism in motion.

- √ The Victim experiences themselves as having no power and being helpless to impact anything.

- √ The Self-Protector experiences a sense of power through controlling others with fear, intimidation or withdrawal.

- √ The Rescuer experiences a sense of power through controlling others with care taking and placating behaviors.

- √ All of the positions are motivated by an immediate need for survival with no real understanding of another's situation or feelings.

CHAPTER 4

Making the Shift to Empowerment

Shifting Out of Blame

Blame drives the Cycle of Egocentrism and keeps us stuck in its pre-defined roles. Our instinct is to find blame. We look for the cause of a problem in order to find a way to control the situation, to either fix it or escape it. This is not a bad thing in and of itself, but it drives us to always assign blame when there is any kind of a problem. This primitive reaction lacks our evolved awareness. Humans have evolved beyond cave dwelling and fighting off (real) tigers for our survival. Yet we continue to think, behave and relate to each other from this place of primitive reactivity. It's time to un-quo the status.

"Knowledge is power" according to Sir Francis Bacon, and I think he was right. Now you have the knowledge. You know that your automatic reactions to perceived threats is a pre-programmed response from your brain to help you survive. Your brain interprets this to mean that you have to behave in certain ways in order to survive the current perceived threat. You can choose to shift into Empowerment rather than choosing to use the illusion of power and control over others.

Empowerment is different than power. Empowerment is discovering that you have inside of you the ability to CHOOSE how you respond to any given circumstance. Discovering how you can respond to a perception of threat from a place of Compassion will empower you to live your life differently. It changes everything.

All of us have heard the word "Compassion" and may even have awareness of what it means, and even be able to practice it in some situations. But it is very different to practice Compassion for others when the others are helpless children in Darfur, or some other group of people who are distant from us and provide no threat. It is entirely different to practice Compassion for those from whom we feel threatened.

How do we do that? How can we drop our defensiveness when we feel threatened and become Compassionate for the person threatening us without becoming endangered ourselves? That is what the Cycle of Compassion is all about.

The Cycle of Compassion

> Compassion is the wish that others be free of suffering. It is by means of Compassion that we aspire to attain enlightenment. To feel true Compassion for all beings, we must remove any partiality from our attitude toward them. Our normal view of others is dominated by fluctuating and discriminating emotions.
>
> - The Dali Lama, 2001

Being Compassionate means being able to see another person as separate and having needs and feelings that have nothing to do with us. We can recognize their pain expressed as their pain, and not a reflection on us. Their feelings are also not ours to change. When we practice Compassion we provide loving support and Empathy from a Respectful place where we own only what is ours and nothing more. Responding Compassionately to others means not judging. It means accepting who they are and trusting them to be doing the best they can, given their situation.

And you don't have to be a Saint or cold and dispassionate to practice it. Compassion is soulful and highly passionate. Without full access to our feelings we cannot be Compassionate.

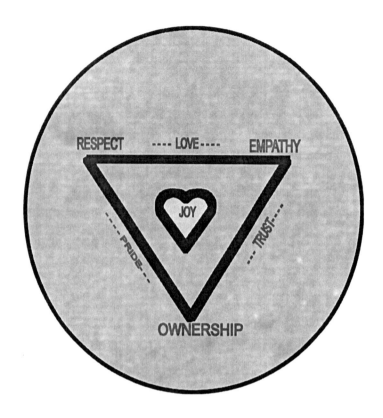

The Cycle of Compassion

Compassion is more than just a feeling: it's action.

The Cycle of Compassion is based on personal empowerment and pride (real pride, not the puffed up false kind) and results in love and aliveness.

Loving ourselves is key to being able to practice Compassion for others. We cannot experience Compassion for others without having achieved it for our selves. In order to understand the grief that others feel we have to allow ourselves to feel our own. We cannot know what grief is, unless we let ourselves feel it! We must experience our own suffering as a distinct, separate self in order to find Compassion for ourselves or another human being's suffering.

After living in the Cycle of Egocentrism, we have to allow in new information about how to live so as to empower ourselves to overcome our biology and experience.

Ownership
Our Sense of Self

To own something means that we cannot be that something. To own our self we must have a self but not be that self. I know this sounds confusing; philosophers spend many thousands of pages trying to explain this concept. The bottom line is that as Victims we do not experience a separate sense of self at all. Anything that happens to us does not feel like it happens separately from what happens to others and vice versa. Without this separate sense of self we lose all sense of Ownership.

When something "bad" happens we are convinced that we are to blame. We believe that we are the badness of what occurred which translates to: we are just plain bad. We let go of any thought that how we feel, who we are, what we want is okay. We even get the sense that we don't really even exist.

Our experience is of living in a world where what we want, how we feel and who we are not only doesn't matter but does not even exist. Even "good" parents can overlook our feelings and needs. The Egocentrism of the adults we needed taught us to disown ourselves in order to comply with their wishes. This happens even when there is no overt abuse or neglect.

There was a story in the paper recently about a young man who was brutally anally raped and beaten by peers in a racially motivated hate crime and left for dead. His classmates and teachers saw him as being resilient and amazingly well adjusted for the two years after the crime. This young man was a bright, likable teen who cheered up the people around him and believed that his pain didn't matter. The story appeared in the paper because the young man jumped off a pier and into the ocean where he subsequently drowned. Even though he had parents that loved him and friends that cared about him, his feelings of not mattering were undoubtedly heightened by his desire to not let anyone worry about him. He avoided his pain by making the people around him happy. But his pain didn't go away. Overlooking his own feelings and needs seemed to be the best way for him to survive the horror of what happened to him. And it appeared to have worked well in the short run.

Our Sense of Control

When we have no sense of self we also lose a sense that we have any ability to impact our lives or circumstances. This is called a "locus of control" loss. When things happen to us as a child (or even as an adult) where we have no control over what happens, we lose contact with the awareness of our own power to impact the outcomes in our world. We sense that we have no control or impact on what happens to us, and that the control over our lives lies outside of ourselves.

The young man in the story above clearly had no sense that he could control what was happening inside of him. He reached a point where he could not longer endure the pain he felt powerless to control.

Regaining Our Self

In order to begin to change that view of others and ourselves we must regain Ownership of our lives and our self. That is a tall order for those deeply entrenched in our Victimhood. It is so frightening that many of us will not be able to do it. We will be so fearful that we will back away and resist movement into Compassion, because the grief seems so enormous that we feel it to be insurmountable. Notice what you are feeling as you contemplate the idea that you alone own responsibility for how you experience your life. Yes, even over your depression, your old unprocessed grief, your financial situation, your fear and anxiety. We own all of it.

> It is not alone what we do, but also what we do not do, for which we are accountable.
>
> - Moliere (1622-1673)

Owning Responsibility

Accountability and Ownership are not blame; blame is

the opposite of Ownership. Blame is a condemnation of a person, attributing all fault with one person, leaving everything else unimpeachable. Victims fear the thought of responsibility because they think it's the same thing as blame. When we blame ourselves we are not taking Ownership, we are being Victims.

Even the young man who was raped had responsibility in what occurred. He was not to blame. He had gotten drunk and fallen in with a group of Nazi Supremacists whom he would never knowingly have associated with had he been sober. That doesn't make it his fault. He didn't know this was going to happen to him!

We all must accept our own part in what occurs in our relationships. One person is never totally to blame for what occurs. As adults, we have choice, therefore responsibility, in what has taken place. We can only own what is ours, not what belongs to another. Owning responsibility means recognizing that we are, at the same time, the Victim, the problem and the solution[4] The need to assign blame disappears when Ownership is assumed. When an experience spins into Egocentrism, anyone involved can call up Respect, Empathy, and Ownership to break the Cycle of Egocentrism. Everyone is responsible for how they relate to others. No one "does it" to the others engaged in the cycle.

This simple truth is often missed; especially when one person is perceived of as being Victimized. To quote Ann Landers, "No one can take advantage of you without your permission."

Choosing to accept Ownership is the opposite of falling

into the Victim position of hopelessness, despair and entrapment. We can change and disown the part of the situation that does not belong to us, without assigning blame. Until we can own our part in the quality of our relationships, we remain Victims. We have freedom of choice over our actions, and we must own our choices and the consequences. Taking Ownership is the willingness to face unappealing truths about ourselves (as well as the appealing ones).[6] When we are stuck in the Victim position, this is extraordinarily difficult because of the tendency to tirades of self-condemnation. Falling into the pit of shame protects us from reproach by others and helps avoid Ownership.

> Man has to be man - by choice; he has to hold his life as a value - by choice; he has to learn to sustain it - by choice; he has to discover the values it requires and practice his virtues - by choice.
>
> - Ayn Rand, "Galt's Speech," Atlas Shrugged

Each of us must learn to own only what is ours, separating our part of the problem from the other's actions and feelings. When we feel someone else is responsible for our happiness, we will feel angry when the other person does not provide bliss. In fact, we own our own unhappiness. Our feelings and responses arise from our personal beliefs, needs, fears, and expectations not from another's behaviors.

Lydia's Story

Riding her scooter to therapy one day, Lydia* was run off the road by a guy in a pickup truck. He never even stopped. She was taken to the ER and complained of a head injury; her helmet had flown off during the crash. Her wrist was broken and her knee had been thrown out of place. During the week in the hospital Lydia began complaining that she couldn't see. Her eyesight was failing for no obvious reason. Over time it was determined that a part of her brain had been injured; the part that controls her eyesight. Lydia, already depressed and struggling now had no vision.

For many people this would have been enough to throw them into a deep depression with no hope of escape – not Lydia. After a period of allowing herself to grieve for her lost vision, Lydia began finding resources for herself. She moved into a home for the blind and learned Braille, though her other head injuries made this particularly difficult. She learned how to use the bus system and to navigate the entire city by herself. Eventually she found someone willing to provide her with a guide dog and training. Before the accident, Lydia had been unemployed; she was too depressed to look for work.

But after she learned to manage her blindness she found a job working in Customer Service for a transportation company. She and her guide dog went to work every day and she earned commendations. She even learned to use a computer with voice recognition technology and was promoted. Within two years she met a man who had been blind since birth and they married and bought a house together. Their son was born two years later. Lydia still works and cares for her child. She hired someone to help her during the day, but she is the primary caretaker of her now 5-year-old son. Lydia had a choice. She could let the blindness keep her from living, or she could take Ownership of her life and move forward. Lydia chose to move forward.

Empathy
Stepping Into Another's Shoes

According to Webster's New International Dictionary third edition (1993), Empathy is "the capacity for participating in or a vicarious experiencing of another's feelings, volitions, or ideas." [7] It is this ability to let ourselves experience another's pain that allows us to let go of the need to be a Self-Protector. We are not feeling the other persons' feelings, we are letting down our boundaries enough to feel what it must be like to be in that other persons' shoes. It is not taking on the other persons' feelings as our own, we still retain a sense of our self, even as we let ourselves see the world from the other persons' eyes for a moment. Empathy recognizes that we are separate and distinct.

Boundaries

Experiencing Empathy means letting our boundaries flex momentarily with a vulnerability that is impossible when we are in the Self-Protective role. When we open our hearts to our own pain we become open to theirs. It is, in fact, the whole reason that we Self-Protectors maintain our rigid shield. When we let down that shield, we allow in awareness of what that other person is feeling. So we have to be open to feelings. The moment we find ourselves opening our hearts to someone that we had formerly considered an enemy, we will feel grief. The grief comes as a result of the awareness of what we have lost. What we have lost is connection with another person. We let our blaming and misunderstanding block us from being in connection. First we feel our own pain, and then we recognize the other persons' suffering.

When we finally get it that we are not bad, wrong or to blame when another becomes upset, we can freely hear the other person's feelings. Suddenly we see the whole picture differently. We see their pain as being about what is going on with them, and not about us at all. We can then react to their pain with Empathy and provide love and support for them to help them through it.

One lovely couple I have worked with is Jim* and Deborah*. Jim was severely neglected and beaten as a child, and Deborah's parents were highly controlling of her. She often gets upset because Jim can't seem to trust what she says to be true. He always has to double check. She gets upset when she forgets that his questioning her has nothing to do with her. During a dialogue Jim was able to express to her that when he was a child his parents were very prejudiced and bigoted against all sorts of people and they told him many things that he later found out were not true. So now, as an adult he instinctively questions anything anyone tells him. Clearly, this has nothing to do with Deborah. Of course, Jim gets very anxious when Deborah gets upset with him and he expects to be beaten. When he really heard Deborah's pain over having never been listened to as a child, he was able to let go of his fear of her and hear that her anger was covering up her pain, and had nothing to do with Jim.

How do you do it?

When you notice someone sounding upset you can say something like, "You sound hurt. What's going on?" or "I heard some anger in that, is there something I did that triggered that?" Again, find your own words, but acknowledge the other person's feelings without taking the blame.

When some one else has expressed feelings to you, responding with Empathy can be simple. Saying something like: "Yeah, I have felt that way before, too. I am sorry you are hurting" helps immensely. Find your own words to let the other person know that you understand how they feel, because you have felt something similar at some time in your life, too.

Opening our hearts to others in this way is a risk. We risk seeing someone else, and being seen by someone else. What if the other person doesn't like what they see? What if the other person attacks us? Before we can come to true Empathy, we must have the boundaries to be able to experience another person's judgments about us as being about the experiences, history and expectations the other person carries, and not really about us. This is the highest form of Respecting another person; to be able to hear their feelings and needs as separate from our own. Recognizing that separateness allows us to own what is ours.

Frank's Story

I met Frank* and Sarah* 20 years into their marriage. She had spent every bit of those 20 years blaming him for being a man. Sarah's father was an angry, violent man who sexually abused her from about the age of seven until she was almost 21. She married Frank in an effort to escape the horrors of her childhood. Initially she had found Frank's attitude of protectiveness comforting and she longed for the safety of his arms. But she was horrified when her children were born; her husband became a man she thought of as angry and sexually pushy. Something about his new role as parent brought out a Self-Protective impulse that she could not control. She berated Frank for any effort he made at parenting and rejected his sexual advances as being "crude" and "awkward." She expressed to him that she believed him only to be interested in her for sex and their sex life died. Frank became depressed and intensely resentful, though he began to believe the things she was telling him.

By the time they came to therapy, Sarah initiated the sessions because she was convinced that Frank needed to be told to change. Frank came in hoping that something might help him save their marriage, because he truly loved his wife, but was beginning to feel there was no escape from the pain except divorce. Eventually, Sarah was able to face her past and separate her abusers from her husband on occasion, but it was difficult for her to see her husband as anything but a perpetrator because in her mind; that's what men were. She softened to him some, but under stress continued to push him into the category of an abuser and could not see herself as anything but a Victim. She never allowed him to discipline their children because she was so afraid of what he might do to them. She convinced their children that he was not a nice person and could not be trusted.

Then she was diagnosed with a second round of breast cancer. Sarah and Frank left therapy and the next time I heard from Frank was a phone call to tell me that she had passed. Two years later, Frank wanted to date again but found himself struggling with anger and problems with his teenaged son, whom he was now raising on his own. His son, Ed* was growing hateful and disRespectful. Frank had gotten him on anti-depressants and they had gone through grief counseling together, but Ed was getting more and more out of control. He was failing in school and not following his father's directions about anything.

Frank knew that Ed was in a lot of pain. He had been working on letting go of his anger toward Sarah and had made a lot of headway in regard to having Empathy for her painful childhood. He had no clue how to help his son who had begun to completely withdraw from communication when he wasn't being angry and disRespectful. Eventually he had a big blowout with Ed. It started when he refused to take his anti-depressants. He threw them down the toilet and began raging at Frank. He spit in his face, and threw a full water bottle at him, hitting him full chest. Frank simply listened as Ed threatened him physically, pushed him down the (short) stairwell and threw a CD player at him.

Frank stayed calm. He remembered what he had learned about not moving into the Self-Protector role and remained empathetic to Ed's pain. He knew the only thing that could help Ed now was for him to continually empathize with Ed's pain. Finally he asked him, "Ed, what is really going on?" Eventually Ed opened up and talked to him about his pain. Ed told Frank that Frank didn't know what it's like to be without a mom, and that he is angry that Frank is dating and that he didn't like any of the women Frank had been seeing. Ed let Frank know that his grief still looms large in his life and that he doesn't know how to live without her. Finally, Ed was able to apologize to Frank and let his father know that he understands his need for companionship. Now Frank and Ed are closer than they have ever been, and Ed no longer views his father as an enemy.

Respect

Doing for Others What They Can and Should Do for Themselves

An early definition of Respect comes from Webster's dictionary (1913).[7] In it Respect is defined as regarding someone with honor. There is no honoring of someone you Rescue. As Rescuers, we act as if we believe the Victim is not capable of being responsible for themselves, As Rescuers, we take over the other person's responsibilities. Aside from infants and mentally incompetent adults, individuals own responsibility for their own personal actions[3]. Doing something for someone else that they can, and should, do for themselves leaves the recipient feeling little and incapable.

Self Respect

We have to start with Self-Respect. Of course we have value

and people can love us for who we are, not just what we do for them! Low self-worth is the root of all of the positions. Rescuers try to get a Respect from others by doing for others; we don't have it inside of our selves. When we believe in, and have confidence in our right to have and share feelings, beliefs and values our sense of worth increases. When we see ourselves as as Rescuer we feel we have to take care of others in order to feel good about ourselves!

Listening to Ourselves and Others

When we Respect others and ourselves we don't give up our own needs, beliefs and values. We can listen to an opposite position without losing our self. It is not the same thing as "giving in" to the other person, in fact "giving in" is a great way to Rescue. Respect is an honest setting aside of one's own position long enough to evaluate the other position's merit. We own our values and beliefs while Respecting other's needs, values and beliefs. By listening and changing, and being aware of our own needs, beliefs and values, we feel even more self-Respect.[4] When we listen we allow ourselves to understand what is really happening so that we can find Empathy for others. This happens when we understand that someone else's view can coexist with ours.

Respect and Trust

When we have a sense of pride in ourselves, we can be Respectful toward others and have confidence that they can and will take responsibility for their behavior.

Respect means not trying to solve someone else's problems.

We trust their ability to resolve the issue without our help. If they ask for help we give support, but we will not "fix it." We do not tell them how we would solve the problem. If they ask, we might make suggestions, but we do not do it for them.

The difference between helping and rescuing may seem subtle. But the difference the person requesting support feels is huge. When we rescue someone, it makes them feel less capable. The message we give them is they are not able to do things well on their own. It keeps them feeling small and disabled.

Karen's Story

Karen's* daddy died when she was only five years old. She recalls pushing on the bathroom door and his body preventing her from opening it. He had been her closest friend and had adored her. Her mother was devastated by the sudden death of her apparently healthy husband of seven years. She was grief stricken and miserable, totally lost in her grief as she tried to rebuild her life. Karen's own grief was never given a second glance. Karen vividly recalls sitting at her father's funeral and thinking, "Who is going to love me?" From that day forward she resolved to get her mother to love her by doing whatever she could to care for her. Her mother responded to her daughter's care taking and grew to expect her daughter to always be there for her. Karen learned that others responded to care taking behaviors, too. She realized she could feel important and valued if she took care of other's needs before her own. She felt loved, but painfully lonely. Shortly after college she met and married her husband, John* who, though he loved her, was unable to communicate his feelings for her. John was a brilliant lawyer who worked in corporate law and had finally made partner as they came into therapy. They had been married almost 20 years, but Karen was finally tired of feeling unappreciated and alone. Their son was almost 15, their daughter 12, and Karen felt drained and exhausted from taking care of her kids, her husband and their home. All of her friends leaned on her, too. She was bright and had returned to school to be a counselor herself. All of her family as well as her friends turned to Karen when they had a problem. Her husband let her do the housework, the child care activities and cooking as well as going to school.

Karen felt she was getting nothing back from anyone, most especially, not from her husband. She was very close to leaving him. John was at a loss, he didn't know anything about what she had been feeling and was confused as to why she was so unhappy. Over time, Karen began to risk telling John what she wanted and needed from him, and he was more than willing to work at doing what she needed. He was hurt that she had never confided in him, but understood that he had been complicit in it by never questioning her needs. He discovered that avoiding problems had been his coping skill as a child that had carried him through to adulthood. In almost 20 years, Karen had never asked him to help her or told him what she needed. She assumed that he didn't care. Karen cried as she told him the simple things that she needed from him, he held her and assured her that he wants her to be happy and that if he had known what she needed he would have always been willing to try.

Still, Karen continued to feel run ragged by her responsibilities with school and with her children. After discussing all the things she did for them in session one day, Karen realized that she was doing things for them that they could and should do for themselves. Though her children were 12 and nearly 15, she still woke them up for school every morning, made their breakfast and took them to school. She picked them up from school (only two blocks from their home) and stayed on top of them while they did their homework. She gathered, washed and folded all their laundry and took them to whatever activities they wanted to attend, even on a moments notice.

After that session, she and John sat both kids down for a serious discussion. Karen apologized to them both for having continued to do things for them as now young adults, that they can and should do for themselves. She let them know that she would no longer be waking them up and fixing them breakfast, nor taking them to and from school (unless the weather was bad) nor doing their laundry, nor standing over their homework. She told them that she knew they are big enough now to do these things for themselves and again apologized for doing things for them they were perfectly capable of doing for themselves. Karen even let them know they would have to give her 24 hours notice if they wanted a ride somewhere, otherwise they would have to get someone else to do it for them. Karen was shocked at their response. They were happy. They immediately stepped up to the plate as if they had been waiting for her to step down. They still tested her with some thing, like forgetting to get up on time, or not turning in homework, but Karen held firm and they took over responsibility for their lives. Karen and John were both delighted to see that their kids were so much more capable than they had ever given them credit for being. Karen finally had time to care for herself and to share intimate moments with her husband that she didn't resent.

Chapter Take Aways

✓ Empowerment is different than power. Empowerment is discovering that you have inside of you the ability to CHOOSE how you respond to any given circumstance.

✓ Discovering how you can respond to a perception of threat from a place of Compassion will empower you to live your life differently. It changes everything.

✓ Compassion is more than a feeling: its action.

✓ We cannot experience Compassion for others without having achieved it for our self.

✓ In order to begin to change that view of others and ourselves we must regain Ownership of our lives and our self.

✓ Empathy is the capacity to vicariously experience another's pain and it allows us to let go of the need for assuming the Self-Protector role.

✓ Respect starts with Self-Respect.

✓ Doing something for someone else that they can, and should, do for themselves leaves the recipient feeling little and incapable.

CHAPTER 5

How we make the shift

Opening to feelings

In essence we are our feelings, far more than our thoughts or what we do. Listening to our feelings we learn about our needs, our desires, our pleasures, what is right in our world and what is not. Without the capacity to feel and express what is happening on an emotional level we are blocked from knowing ourselves.

Ever known anyone that was so shut off from their feelings that they could not tell you how they felt about anything? So much of the time when you ask someone what they feel about something they will tell you what they think! They say, "I feel judged" or "I feel misunderstood." Think those are feelings? Think again! Feelings are felt in your body. "Misunderstanding" and "judging" are head activities. A feeling is something related to: sad, mad, scared or happy. Letting yourself be aware of what your body tells you frees you to know yourself.

Letting ourselves feel the feelings of pain, anxiety, fear, anger, despair and hopelessness creates a dilemma. People say to me, "What do I do with those feelings?" The only thing you need to "do" with your feelings is to "have them." We need to learn how to feel, identify, and express them.

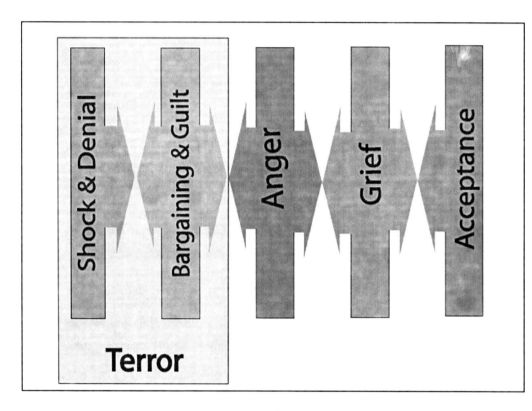

The Wall of Grief

You undoubtedly know what grief is, it's layers of feelings that come with loss. It's funny, but grief can come with any type of loss. I remember losing my keys one morning when my kids were little and I was late for work. It was summer time, and it was a Monday morning. They had just had two days of play with their dad and me by the pool in the apartment where we lived. When I discovered I didn't know where they were I said "I can't believe I have misplaced my keys!" (shock and denial). Then I asked the kids, "Have you seen my keys?" (bargaining). Growing more frustrated I felt really angry and started shouting "I've got to find my keys!" (anger). Then, I started to cry (grief). Then my stepson (two at the time) dug behind the couch and pulled out my keys!

But we also have more intense kinds of losses that we tend to avoid.

No matter who we are, we have a natural tendency to avoid pain. It's a human trait- the avoidance of pain is as natural as breathing. We see a sizzling grill; some part of us instinctively contracts in fear. So it is with grief. Most of us avoid allowing ourselves to fall into the depths of the pain that grieving entails. "Crying about it won't change it" or "Tears won't bring it back" are warnings that we often hear from our parents and pass on to our children. We begin the legacy of unexpressed grief from the moment we hold our breath and brace our diaphragm against the waves of pain resulting from the loss.

What we are losing

All of our lives we have depended on the Cycle of Egocentrism to assign meaning and to ascertain a course of action. We have always depended on this old paradigm to understand what is happening and to make sense of our world. Changing to a new way of perceiving our lives and our selves is terrifying. What will this mean? What do we do now? How will I cope without the old structured way that sheltered me from my feelings?

What we are losing is our way of understanding and making meaning. What does that mean about our past? How do we now make sense of and justify our actions? Losing our old way of perceiving our world and our selves is a category five experience. It wracks our very sense of who and what we are. To give up the things that we have hung our identity on, that we have hung our entire meaning structure upon is scary, even terrifying.

It's a scary and painful process to realize that everything we thought was true is not true. The grief can feel really powerful. But the end result is that we feel less separate from others. We express the kind of Compassion that Jesus taught. We accept ourselves wholly and completely. We let go of judgment of others. We feel deeply connected to others no matter how badly they behave, because we now understand why they act the way they do, and we have Compassion for them.

Phases of Grief
Terror

The first thing we feel is terror. This is the natural tendency of humans to retract from pain or perceived pain. Terror says, "Oh, I'd better not go there." It makes us want to pull away, avoid the pain, repress it or dissociate ourselves from it. Most of the time, most of us will immediately retreat back into the Cycle of Egocentrism because anything else is too scary.

Our well-meaning parents and family members who are terrified of their own feelings model this for us, teaching it to us in an unconscious way. Or a subtle form of invalidation can accomplish it. John Bradshaw (1992), in **Creating Love**, uses the example of a little boy dressed up like a cowboy asking everyone "Are you a cowboy?"[8] When he asks his father his father says, "Are you a cowboy?" The boy replies, "Yes" to which the father says, "Well, real cowboys are not afraid!" The child responds by feeling confused and then as if something is wrong with him because he does feel afraid. In order to maintain a sense of connection with his father the child must disown his fear, separating a part of himself from the whole of himself, his feelings and his world. Afterwards the child will develop a phobia of feeling his fear or any other feeling that connects him to himself.

Walking through the terror is not for the light of heart. It's what makes the entire process of changing paradigms from the Cycle of Egocentrism into the Cycle of Compassion so difficult.

Shock and Denial

Shock is the first sign of the terror. Our heart rate goes up and we go into disbelief. Then we start to feel numb psychologically, as well as in our bodies. Then we start to deny reality. Thoughts like "This can't be happening" or "No, not this" run through our heads. The feeling of numbness can feel so uncomfortable over time that we are driven to behave in dangerous ways. It's why people cut on themselves and engage in risk taking activities like drag racing and street fighting. When it's prolonged people will do almost anything to feel again (except face the grief).

Bargaining and Guilt

The second part of the terror is "Bargaining and Guilt." This is when reality starts to set in, and you begin to accept that it is possible that your whole life has been ruled by something more powerful than your own intentions. At this point, the struggle is to remain out of the Victim position. Guilt has a powerful pull to return to the Cycle of Egocentrism because it brings up those shame feelings. Guilt is not the same as shame, and can be tolerated and worked through in a rational and adult manner. But for most of us, moving into experiencing the guilt for what we have done without shifting back into the shaming blaming Victim role is a difficult maneuver.

Linda's Story

Linda* had been raised by a mother who was extremely narcissistic. Linda's mother was so focused on herself that the only way Linda had any hope of being noticed was to do things for her. Excelling in school got her nothing, but doing chores for her mother got her affirmations. Taking care of her siblings when her mother was tired, feeding the dog, scrubbing the floors and making dinner for the family won her some bits of approval. She learned that others responded well to her care taking, too. She "helped" friends with their homework by doing it for them. Linda even did chores for her friends, and they eagerly allowed her to do it. When Linda began to see that her Rescuing behaviors had been for the purpose of getting approval by others she was devastated. "But this means that everything I have done is a lie! That all I have ever done is to manipulate and control others, when I thought I was trying to help people. How can I learn to accept anything good about myself when you say I am so bad!" To accept that she was a part of the Cycle meant that Linda had to let go of all the old concepts of "bad" and "good" about herself and others. At first, this was too much for her to comprehend. She continued to struggle with denial of her own part in the Cycle, simply because to do so would mean letting go of believing that she is "bad." She shook in terror at the thought of changing the core by which she had lived her life. For her, the idea that someone had to be to blame (usually her) was the foundation of her belief system. Changing this would shake up her belief system about her entire life. Her terror was of losing the image that she had of her parents as being attentive and available. Believing that she was "bad" was much safer.

Anger

> How often it is that the angry man rages denial of what his inner self is telling him.
>
> - Frank Herbert

The anger we feel during healing has a different quality than that experienced in the Cycle of Egocentrism. The difference is that the anger expressed as a Rescuer or Self-Protector never gets spent, it is self-perpetuating. It is self-perpetuating because any time we, or someone else, gets hurt by our anger, the anger continues. Anger from the Cycle of Egocentrism is focused on a target and is about revenge or retribution.

The anger that we express through the healing process of moving into the Cycle of Compassion is released as a fury over wounding that should never have taken place. It is not about wanting to harm or blame someone.

When we express our anger with Compassion it includes full awareness that the person who wounded us was also wounded, and it is with full awareness of the wrongness of the other person's wounding, too. Compassionate anger is directed at events, not at people.

Edmonds' Story

Eddmond* was a Rescuer 95% of the time. He spent all his energy doing nice things for other's, including his mother. His mother had berated him during his adolescence for being "too fat" and raged at him for not cleaning their home well enough after his parent's divorce. This constant barrage of anger lodged against Richard turned him into a quiet, compliant child who never stood up to anyone, and always did what anyone asked of him. As a young adult he had a successful career as a teacher, but he spent his weekends looking after his mother. He began having fits of rage with his roommate after spending Saturdays with his Mother.

Afterwards he felt more angry, out of control and remorseful, with no clue as to why he had treated his friend this way. During therapy he began to connect with the intense anger he had toward his mother for her treatment of him and his roommate encouraged him to have a "confrontation" session with her. Many psychotherapists would have agreed with this and set one up as soon as Richard felt strong enough. Instead, Edmond worked through his anger in session using various techniques for connecting with the hurt and pain as well. Finally, he looked up and said, "My God, what could have happened to my mother to have made her behave like that?" He began to cry and connect with the anger at whatever it was that happened to his mother to create that kind of rage inside of her. He was able to allow himself to have Empathy for her, without excusing her behavior. Then he was ready for a session with his mother that was not a "confrontation" but a clearing of communication and a chance for an honest connection with her.

Grief

Understanding that the way to Compassion is to work through the pain is not enough to get us through it. Most people become so overwhelmed and frightened that they cannot imagine working through their unprocessed grief. When I talk to people I see a panic in their eyes that asks, "Do you mean I have to feel stuff?" From childhood we have been taught that it is better to ignore, pretend, medicate, distract and deny pain than experience it. Yet, like any wound, if it is not allowed to drain, it will become infected and cause us to become quite ill.

The sad part is that holding back such an immense amount of emotions takes an incredible amount of energy. What I had to learn is that emotions are really "energy in motion," and to hold back an onslaught of feelings requires a great deal of strength. Releasing feelings actually frees up a tremendous amount of energy. We expend so much effort holding our breath, clenching our jaw, swallowing down, "shouldering" and "bucking up" that we have little left for enjoying our life. To a great extent, this is why people spend so much money on "relaxation." Alcohol, tranquilizers, and marijuana are but a few of crutches we use to escape the tension.

So how do we do it, after spending a lifetime to learn how to not feel, how do we learn to let it out? There is no right way for any one person. Each of us has to find our own path and discover where and how they can find release.

Debbie's Story

At six, Debbie* moved to Florida to live with her mother as she started her new job as a Ballet instructor at a large arts center. Her father had opted to remain at his well paying job in Texas while he looked for work in his field in Florida. Debbie's mother had a brief bout of breast cancer when Debbie was four, but her mother had gone into remission and there was no reason to fear for her health. But one year after moving to Florida, her mother's cancer reappeared. Alone in Florida, with no family and few friends, Debbie's mother relied on Debbie to care for her. At seven, Debbie learned to call the Doctor to make appointments, to call acquaintances to secure rides to the appointments, to make meals for them both and to get herself to her school and events as she needed. Debbie recalls wanting desperately for her mother to get better and not minding doing anything for her. Eventually, when Debbie was 12, her mother became ill enough that she was forced to give up her job and return to Texas. Within weeks, her mother went to hospice care and Debbie waited for her mother to die. The day that her mother died, her father asked her to come in to the hospice facility to see her mother. Debbie couldn't bear the thought of seeing her on her deathbed, and refused. Her father was angry with her initially, and even more so when her mother died later that day.

Debbie recalls the funeral and the reception at their home afterwards as if walking through a cloud. She says she didn't cry, didn't feel anything. During the reception she remained in her room in the basement and no one even came and checked on her. The day following the funeral she returned to school and everyone commented on how well she was handling everything in the weeks that followed.

Finishing High School early, Debbie went on to get her nursing degree and easily found employment as an ICU nurse. Two years into her first job she began having panic attacks at work, she didn't know why. Every day she watched people die and remained her professional self, but suddenly she found herself thrown into panic at moments she did not understand.

Entering therapy she discovered that the grief over her mothers' death had remained inside of her encapsulated, waiting for her to have the emotional maturity and support to deal with it. Debbie found it hard to let people be there for her, as she had always been in the Rescuer role, and never relied on anyone. Yet she realized that she had to lean on friends if she was to survive the intensity of the grief she held inside. After several months of working on releasing her grief and processing through her sense of guilt for not saving her mother, Debbie was able to return to work. She still has bouts of crying when certain anniversary dates hit, she says, but the panic is gone and the grief is not so overwhelming as to prevent her from working.

Acceptance

Acceptance is not a destination, it is a part of the process in the same way that all the other phases of grief are. We will come in and out of acceptance as the process of grief continues. We know we are there when we hear ourselves saying things like "I realize that my parents did the best they could, with what they had available." And "I can forgive myself, because I was doing the best I could at the time. I didn't know any other way to survive."

There is a sense of relief of tension when we move into this phase of our grief work. We stop struggling against what we know to be true. We don't blame anyone or anything; we are able to let go of guilt, shame and shock. What generally remains is a sadness that is not overwhelming- it is perhaps even bittersweet. We can own what occurred as being a part of the whole of our lives, the good and the bad of it. We can own our own part in whatever occurred, (perhaps with laughter) and see how others contributed, without blame.

Acceptance indicates a thought process that includes a new idea of who we are now, a new definition of our self. Sometimes that includes becoming an activist or a participant in a support group to help others through the kind of loss that we just maneuvered our way through. Whatever results, we have learned to carry a piece of that person or event with us with a new frame, seeing ourselves, the situation and the people involved in a whole new perspective.

Most of all, acceptance is a place of Compassion for others and ourselves.

Mary's Story

In 1999, Mary's* teenaged son was found dead having accidentally frozen his lungs while inhaling propane. Mary, her husband and her children were devastated. But Mary had been the Rescuer in the family and spent all of her energy after the funeral in caring for her other children. She turned her focus to them and to making sure that each of them processed their grief in a healthy way and survived the tragedy without too much scaring. Her husband, Larry was severely depressed afterwards and she made sure that he got the medical attention he needed. He started into therapy and on anti-depressants to help him deal with the pain he was in three years after his son's death.

After Mary was certain that everyone else was getting what they needed and well on their way to recovery. She collapsed while grocery shopping for the family four years to the day after her son died. Mary came into therapy begrudgingly. She didn't need help she said, it was just a mild episode. But after learning how her Rescuing had prevented her from confronting her own grief, Mary began to open up.

Her defensiveness and fear regarding facing the pain, she realized, came from her sense of guilt. She believed that her son used the propane because she hadn't been a good enough mother. Her guilt blocked her ability to face the grief. Once she allowed the grief she could barely function. Her family came to her support, and she reluctantly allowed them to take over some of her daily duties for a while as she let herself deal with the long delayed grief.

During the time she had not faced her grief she realized that part of the problem was that she had no one with whom she felt comfortable discussing her loss. Mary began researching support groups for parents and found little help available. She decided to launch a Web site to help her connect with other parents whom had lost children to drugs. Her Web site brought her new friends and gave her and others people she could talk to about her loss. The web site has initiated after school programs and education classes that have spread all over the world. Mary still feels sad when she remembers her son, but now she can talk about him and has a sense of peace about what happened to him. She no longer blames herself, or him.

The Gift of our grief

The internal transformation of becoming alive

As children, most of us were never taught how to manage our feelings. Our feelings were just something we were "stuck with," and we were left on our own to manage them. "Stop crying! Don't be sad. Don't take that tone with me." We learned to treat our emotions as an unfortunate chronic disease. We never really learned how to cope with them. Though the truthful identification and expression of feelings is seldom directly addressed in our families of origin, we witness how others in our lives manage feelings. We copy the behavior of important role models. We watch our parents and mentors. We see them manage or mismanage their emotions and follow suit. Stoic parents often create stoic children. Alcoholic parents often create alcoholic children. Abusive parents often create abusive children. Passive aggressive parents often create passive aggressive children. The culture of our childhood creates the way we cope with our emotions. We learn to cope emotionally in a sick way or in a healthy way.

We learn to cope by doing whatever we can to not feel. We push the feelings down, we avoid them through work or activity, and we push them out of our thoughts and our body awareness. All of which move us away from feeling anything. Our feelings become blunted and we walk through life numb and half alive.

What are emotions?

Emotions are not a disease, nor are they something to be avoided. Though emotions should not always be indulged, since indulging in our emotions is not the same thing as allowing ourselves to process them. The "Me" movement of the 1980's in therapy encouraged confrontation and vigorous expression of feeling, especially to those labeled as perpetrators. It was painful for me to witness clients and friends who participated in the therapy of that time divorce their spouses and lose contact with family members. At that time, it seemed in vogue to inform others in any manner: "You are not letting me have my feelings!" The assumption seemed to be that any way of expressing feelings should be acceptable. I heard from my client's partners stories of yelling, whining and even verbally abuse in the name of: "I'm just sharing my feelings!"

Emotions provide information-information about our world. In the same way our physical senses provide information, our emotions also provide information to the body. Our survival and safety depends upon the information we gather from the world around us. Our eyes tell us size, color, shape, texture and place of objects. Our ears tell us what is happening around us-the things around us that we cannot see. They give us the location of objects and inform of the possibility of danger versus safety. Our sense of touch also delineates between danger and safety. Touch provides information about fun. Touch also lets us know what is good for us physically and what is detrimental to our physical safety. Our sense of taste tells us what is healthy for us and what is not. Even though, sugar and spices can often fool us. Our sense of smell bombards us with a variety of information about the world. Smell can tell us who is attractive and who should be avoided. Smell also alerts the need for safety. When fire or other noxious fumes occur, we know to get away. Smells also bring good memories of the bakery shop or Sunday dinner, and smell invites us to eat something scrumptious.

Emotions are like another set of senses. Emotions gather and present us with important information about our world.

How we learn about emotions

Typical families provide little training in emotional development. As we grew up in our families of origin, we did not learn how to appropriately interpret emotional information. Because we were taught to "be good" or "behave," we generally get our wires crossed. Our reactions to what we feel emotionally do not necessarily match the situation. And, usually we were not allowed to completely process strong emotions. Unprocessed feelings hang around in our brains and bodies and wait for closure. The result is that we end up confused about what is happening on a subconscious level. Our responses to situations often do not make logical sense. No wonder people choose to avoid, medicate, repress and dissociate from messy feelings!

The benefits of feelings

If we learn how to make sense of them, emotions are an endless, rich resource. Our feelings are experienced in our bodies. Our bodies contain all the wisdom we need to process our feelings, if we listen. To begin, we must learn how to interpret our feelings, and how to respond and express them in healthy ways.

Taking the time to honor the pain, courage and energy it takes to transform yourself into new ways of being is key to self nurturing. Be patient with yourself and understand that you are in the beginning stages of becoming fully alive.

How do we change?
Connections with others

Human beings are formed and supported through connections with others. There was a time in psychology where we thought that the imaginary goal for human beings was to be completely independent. What we found is that independence is not the ideal. Yes, we need to be able to manage without support, if need be, in order to survive. But to be independent when there is no need-is to be cut off from others. A person capable of what we now refer to as "interdependence" is the healthier person. To be able to lean on another when necessary, and to be leaned upon when that is necessary, is the ideal. But developing the ability to be interdependent is fraught with all of the things that keep a person stuck in the Cycle of Egocentrism.

Connecting with ourselves

In order to be fully functioning interdependent person we must be connected first to ourselves, and then have the ability to be connected to others. Sometimes these two things will occur simultaneously, as in therapy, or in a good marriage or friendship. Most of the time, we are alone when we begin this journey, if not in actuality, then in practicality. When I began this journey I was married, but I was unable to connect with my partner, or myself. At the time, the Cycle of Compassion was not understood. My therapists, however well intentioned, vilified my husband and pushed us further apart. They did similar things with my family. I had friends, but because of my inability to connect, I was not able to connect with them on a deep level. I was, as you may well be, essentially alone as I began the process of discovering how to live differently.

You need to start where you are, with what you have available to you. You may not be connected to anyone at the moment. You may have some people around you but do not know how to connect, or feel that they are not the people with whom you want to connect. It does not need to stop you from finding out who you really are, and walking through the years of unprocessed grief you likely have inside.

Honoring ourselves with our humanity

The pain of loss associated with grief feels like Victimization. It is easy to confuse being in a Victim state with feeling a great deal of grief. However, it is not the same thing. Shame is a key factor. In the Victim place, we are in so much shame that we cannot allow ourselves to process through the pain. In the Victim place, neither can we get the kind of healthy support needed to move through the grief. We seek out people, things, or situations to move us away from our feelings. We languish in self-hatred rather than self-nurturing. We will not allow ourselves to fully express the grief. Remember that blame blocks the grieving process. Self-hatred causes us to blame ourselves for everything that is wrong with the world around us and within ourselves. Self-hatred is the epitome of blame. Allowing ourselves to face our grief is a choice, an action. Victims do not take action; they are stuck in the blame, shame, and despair. Victims do not move through the full range of emotions in grieving.

Leaning to Love Ourselves

In walking through the Wall of Grief, we learn to love ourselves enough to process our emotions. We can work through all the repressed emotions felt by our precious inner child. We begin feeling and are eager to discover the gifts those feelings hold for us. We do not find ways to get "control" of the feelings. We do not find ways to "escape" the feelings. We do not look for anyone to "blame" for the feelings. Those behaviors revert us back to Rescuing or Self-Protecting.

Taking Ownership

As we begin to move into the Cycle of Compassion, we take Ownership of what is happening. We Respect our own ability to manage feelings, and we practice Self–Empathy. That means loving ourselves just as we love others that are precious to us. That means recognizing the perfect, lovable child inside of us and treating ourselves with the same loving kindness we do the other people that we love.

When we no longer have to block the feelings of pain, anxiety, fear, anger, despair and hopelessness. We let ourselves fully express them. Below are some of the ways we can process through the feelings associated with grief.

Processes we can use

Meditating Developing Our Internal Witness

Key to progressing through Wall of Grief is developing an internal "Witness." Numerous books of philosophy address this topic, and many (at least in my opinion) are difficult to read and even harder to fully comprehend. I will try to make the idea simple and easy to grasp.

An Internal Witness is a part of the self. The Internal Witness stands back and watches. Our Internal Witness keeps a record of everything that we are feeling, doing, and experiencing. Like a computer that makes no judgment, our Internal Witness makes no judgments. The Internal Witness does not attempt to change the experience. This all-accepting presence inside of us is interested in what is happening but is objectively separate. We all have the capacity to develop an unconditional Internal Witness, and it is not actually that difficult to achieve.

Developing this Internal Witness aspect of ourselves teaches us that the essence of who we are is separate from what we experience in our lives. Our experience becomes something we have, deeply and honestly. But, who we are in total is so much more. We can allow ourselves the experience of our pain and our joys without identifying our sense of self with that experience. We are not our pain. We are not our joy. We are a spirit separate from these experiences. Our spirit is able to have our experiences without identifying with them.

This process is important because we stop judging our experiences as being "bad or good," our "fault" or even our "credit." Our experience simply is what it is, without judgment. The duality of right and wrong, good and bad becomes less important, and we simply "are" in our experience from a place of loving acceptance.

The most common way to develop an Internal Witness is to meditate. For those of us with anxiety, meditation is not always an easy thing to do. However, it often makes the biggest difference in our experience of our life. Setting aside time to Witness our own experience through meditation is a gift of self-love that is immeasurably valuable.

There is a Zen concept called "Mindfulness" that is valuable in helping us establish our Internal Witness. In Mindfulness we are able to pull into ourselves and notice what we are thinking, feeling, and experiencing in a quiet, meditative experience.

Some time when you have plenty of time to sit with your self, create a nurturing environment. Put on some soothing music if you would like. Begin breathing. Put your hand on your belly and breathe so that as you take in breath your belly rises. Slowly fill your belly completely up with air. Open your mouth and slowly let the air out. Repeat this for several minutes. See if you can continue breathing in this way for 15 minutes or so. Sit with yourself and just notice how it feels in your body now and what emotions are present. Sometimes people will have tears come up, others racing heartbeat, some heavy pain in their chest or stomach. See if you can let yourself have whatever experience you are having without judging it, but simply noticing what is happening and allowing it to continue. Write about what this is like for you. Repeat this exercise daily if possible

Exforming

In InterPlay™ a form of improvisational movement, storytelling and sound, we use a process called "Exforming." Exforming helps us to "get it out." Getting it out can take many forms. This can be in words (storytelling, song, poetry, dramatic writing, prose), through a visual art (painting, drawing, sculpting, film) or through movement (dance, movement improvisation) or some combination of these. Exforming can be done alone, and it often is. However, in my experience, it is most powerful when done in the presence of supportive others. We need others to recognize our life experience. Sharing our stories, our poetry, our pictures, our dance and our song with others allows us to feel heard, perhaps even understood.

Containing

Sometimes feelings overwhelm us, and we are consumed with the feeling of "this is too much." It may feel necessary to "escape" them in order to feel settled. But, it is not. We need to find a way to "take a break" from them until the intensity passes. This is containment. Containment is when we find a way to feel enjoyment and nurturance, in the midst of our pain. We must find behaviors that do not also harm us. We have to come up with a list of things that we can do when we feel overwhelmed that will take good care of us and help us feel nourished.

We pay attention to what our bodies need, allowing ourselves to have our feelings even as we do the other activities. Staying in our "Stuff" too long can be counter-productive. This does not mean reverting to addictive measures to avoid feeling. What it does mean is finding new behaviors. Find someone to be with or something that makes us laugh. Nurturance moves us out of the pits of despair.

Using your support

When we are in the process of opening up our hearts to old, shut off pain such as anger and fear, support is imperative. We need to let those closest to us know that we are having a temporarily difficult time. We can even stretch to let people we feel safe with (even those that we may not know that well) know that we are working through some tough things. We do not have to give intimate details of our lives, but we do need to let safe others know that we are distressed. Support comes in many ways. We need at least one other person with whom we can talk to in depth. Support means finding people who will allow us to cry, people with whom we can laugh and play. We need others that will help us "contain" and still others that can give us nurturing. I remember one girlfriend who was not particularly good at giving verbal support, she just sat with me and did my nails, and another friend took me out dancing. Both were marvelous examples of support.

Nurturing ourselves

There are hundreds of ways to nurture, but if no one taught us how to do so, we may find ourselves perplexed. What feels nurturing to me? How do I nurture myself? These questions may be difficult to answer. Ask your friends what they do for nurturance. Pay attention to what feels (physically and emotionally) good to you. What did you do as a child that felt good? When I was little, I went for walks. I played on the swings in the playgrounds. I found something I could create (unconsciously "exforming"). I baked. I called it "making stuff." As I grew older, I wrote poetry. Explore what feels nurturing for you. For some people long baths, candles and music helps. Some like to snuggle in pajamas and "read stories." Other people I know like watching old cartoons from their childhood. Others draw using kindergarten crayons using their non-dominant hand.

Putting it all together

When you let yourself do the things that are going to help you heal, you are practicing Ownership a the highest level. Internal healing moves you, your family, co-workers, community and the world toward the practice of Compassion.

Chapter Take Aways

- √ Grief is the wall of emotion we must travel through to heal the wounds life has dealt us.

- √ There is a bottom. The pain is not limitless. The thing we most fear, being stuck in that deep despair; is not going to happen.

- √ No matter who we are, we have a natural tendency to avoid pain. It's a human trait-the avoidance of pain is as natural as breathing.

- √ Terror starts from our natural tendency as humans to retract from pain or perceived pain.

- √ Anger that is experienced and expressed through the healing process of moving into the Cycle of Compassion is not targeted in an attempt to harm or blame someone.

- √ Each of us has to find our own path and discover where and how you can find release.

- √ Grief, like any wound, if it is not allowed to drain will become infected and cause us to become quite ill.

CHAPTER 6

The Shift Into Compassion

Compassion

The Mechanics of Compassion

- The opposite of the Cycle of Egocentrism is the Cycle of Compassion.

- Empathy is the opposite of Self-Protecting.

- Respect is the opposite of Rescuing.

- Ownership is the opposite of being a Victim.

When we apply these to the conflicts in our lives, we shift into living our lives differently. The key to having success from the inside is practicing Compassion for others and ourselves.

You see, this whole system of the Cycle of Egocentrism happens first inside. Think about it, what do you do when you are helpless and powerless? When you have had a really hard day and feel out of control? You look around for something to get you out of feeling that. And we all have our favorites. My personal favorite is shopping. For others it's alcohol, or TV, or food, or even sex. What happens is that we eventually end up hurting ourselves by using whatever it is we used to stop the powerlessness, we end up being powerless over the very thing we used to avoid feeling powerless.

What is Compassion?

> Compassion is not religious business, it is human business, it is not luxury, it is essential for our own peace and mental stability, it is essential for human survival.
>
> - Dali Lama

When we are Compassionate, we experience others as fully separate beings with their own needs, wants and pain. We can recognize pain expressed to us by others, is their pain, and not a reflection upon who we are and not ours to change. We provide loving support and Empathy from a Respectful place where we own only what is ours and nothing more. Responding Compassionately to others means not judging. It means accepting who they are and trusting them to be doing the best they can, given their situation.

This may sound like something only a monk or a saint is capable of doing. Most assuredly, this is not about being a perfect person, or a person who is cold and devoid of emotional responses to others.

Compassion is soulful and highly passionate. Without full access to our feelings we cannot be Compassionate. Compassion is as much a feeling as it is action.

This is, of course, what we aspire to on our many spiritual paths, but it's so hard to achieve and to stay true to ourselves at the same time. Compassion is not giving to others while not giving to ourselves. It is not giving to others while carrying a burden of resentment or jealousy. Compassion is not out of the goodness of our heart. It is the goodness of our hearts.

In experiencing true Compassion, we feel warm and caring and yet do not feel compelled to jump in and rescue, fix or try to heal them. We are still there for people if they reach out to us in any way; but we are secure enough in ourselves to not use fixing them to fill our own emptiness.[6]

Compassion is fully and completely in the present and not in assumptions and fantasies that occur within our irrational mind. We are present with what is now, in the moment. From Compassion we respond to others with authenticity. Our inside thoughts and feelings are reflected in our outside words and actions. We are consistent and congruent.

Becoming aware

Before anyone can change, they must first become aware of

the problem. Once we understand that we are not to blame, and in fact, no one really is to blame, we can start the process of moving into doing things differently. We do the best we can at the process. We cannot be expected to do better than we can.

Of course just having the information about how we engage in the drama doesn't change it. We have to know how and we have to practice the actions. We have to have patience and we have to work at it consciously and with Empathy for ourselves in the process. We also need support and the emotional space to allow ourselves to heal the grief that we will feel as we move into the Wall of Grief. It might mean finding a support group or therapy. Some of us will be able to find the support we need in our current relationships.

Acceptance of what is

Through accepting our own pain, we begin to recognize other's pain and give ourselves, and others, the space to not be perfect. The world is not divided into perfect and bad. In fact, perfect doesn't exist so the world is not divided at all and everything that is less than perfect, even okay, good, great, etc. is included in it. This allows us to accept that all of us are doing the best we can with what we have.

At the core of Egocentrism is pain. Pain is what drives the cycle, and it is the result of the cycle. Players in each of the roles in Egocentrism experience pain in relations with others and ourselves. We must find ways to cope with the pain that brings about more pain. In this classic addiction cycle, we use people, drugs or find activities to medicate our pain while at the time creating more pain for others and ourselves.

Our capacity for Joy

The good news is that Compassion allows us to experience joy. Compassion is in fact driven by our capacity for joy. Closing ourselves off from our capacity for joy by medicating our pain stops us from the possibility of experiencing joy. It is impossible to experience joy or pleasure without also being able to experience our pain. Our fear of processing the pain keeps us from moving into the experience of joy.

When we hit the terror at the top of the Wall of Grief, we don't think we can do it so we medicate, and that is what stops us from moving into joy.

> ...ye shall be sorrowful, but your sorrow shall be turned into joy.
>
> - John, 16:22 St. James Bible

Moving through the pain

The process is at first terrible. We feel terrified and small. We feel miserable and fear that there is no way out of the intense fear, grief, and anger that we feel. It feels bottomless and hopeless. But it is not bottomless, or hopeless. It is the key to hope. Only movement from Egocentrism to Compassion will allow us to experience joy.

How the Cycle of Compassion works

The positions of the Cycle of Compassion are interdependent. They work together in unison to make the cycle work.

- Empathy without Respect becomes pity, without Ownership becomes condescension.
- Ownership without Empathy becomes narcissism, without Respect becomes intrusion.
- Respect without Empathy becomes aloofness, without Ownership becomes arrogance.

To achieve Compassion, we must also have Respect, Empathy and Ownership active in our interactions with others and ourselves. No single corner of the Cycle of Compassion can pathe the way out of Egocentrism. But with all three corners together, we move into a new paradigm.

Through true Compassion we find our way to experience joy in our relationships.

Joy then becomes our driving force. We refuse to revert back to the old Egocentrism patterns because we now know that joy is possible.

We find that love, trust and confidence provide us with a deep sense of meaning and purpose. We may not always be "happy" with the events or circumstances that life hands us, but we will continue to find meaning and purpose in our lives.

The Process of Becoming Compassionate

Becoming Compassionate is a delicate process. It starts with accepting that we are all basically the same and that our automatic responses can be changed. The second step is to open our hearts to the possibility that we can see ourselves as lovable, worthy human beings. The Victim position, from which the other positions in the Cycle of Egocentrism are derived, is at core the position of shame. Learning to forgive ourselves and have Empathy for ourselves will allow us to recognize the basic goodness of others as well.

But it is not an easy process. Our instinctive emotional responses are painfully strong and often irresistible. The instincts our brain insists we use are compelling. When we have needs that were not met in childhood they compel us to remain in a stance that demands that we get those needs met before we can move out of blame and shame.

Our only hope is to overcome our instincts and act with Compassion.

Jenny and Gary's Story

Jenny* was a 40-year-old mom with two kids and a serious problem with Rescuing. She took care of everyone and everything other than herself. She never asked for help and resented her husband for not pitching in and doing more in terms of housework and childcare. Gary* was a brilliant engineer and he had just made partner at the firm where he worked. He had a history of drinking too much too much when they were first married and disappearing until late into the night with no accounting for his whereabouts when he returned home. Jenny had such a backlog of resentment toward Gary that when she finished her graduate program she was ready to divorce him. They hardly spoke and rarely had sexual contact.

Therapy started with Jenny. She began the process of recognizing her own shame and pain and how she had been trained to be her mothers' Rescuer since she was less than five years old. She grieved for this little girl and began feeling a desire for closeness with her husband. She didn't think it was possible, but she didn't want her kids to have to suffer through a divorce and it's consequences, so she invited him to therapy.

To Jenny's surprise, Gary was very willing to work in therapy. He was scared of losing her and he, too, didn't want to go through a divorce. The process was hard for Gary. He tended to Self-Protect by burying himself in work, by withdrawing physically and emotionally, and intellectualizing. Many times in therapy Jenny would grow frustrated with him because of his avoidance. But eventually, Gary began to connect with how hard it was to be a smart, nerdy kid unable to defend himself against the athletic tough guys in school. He became aware of how hard it was for him to have a self in his family with his very overbearing mother. Sharing this pain with Jenny allowed her to move into Empathy for his behavior.

Jenny started letting go of her Rescuing behaviors and felt

less resentment toward Gary and he softened toward her and began being affectionate with her. They began to play together, going out on dates and taking dancing lessons. Now divorce is off the table. They both have reconnected with a deep sense of joy in their relationship. They still have work to do, as they process through the grief that remains, but they are well on their way to experiencing their lives and relationship differently.

Compassion for ourselves

> To love is to value. Only a rationally selfish man, a man of self-esteem, is capable of love - because he is the only man capable of holding firm, consistent, uncompromising unbetrayed values. The man who does not value himself, cannot value anything or anyone.
>
> - Ayn Rand, 1932

Compassion has to start with self-love. True Compassion for others cannot exist without having it for our self. And it starts with being able to love ourselves enough to help ourselves through the Wall of Grief. We have to know our own suffering before we can begin to know another's. We must experience our own suffering as a distinct, separate self in order to find Compassion for ourselves or another human being's suffering.

Affirm that I am okay

Fear and shame grab us when we are in the Cycle of Egocentrism. No matter what our automatic reaction, we always start by feeling afraid and ashamed. We lose connection with our adult self and feel unable to defend ourselves. We feel unworthy.

In order to move through this we have to affirm our value as a person. Affirmations can pull us out of our reactivity. At that moment, if we slow down enough (breathing, thinking about who is talking to us), we then remember that our reactivity is not about the present at all. We start to comfort and reassure the child part of us that is having the reaction.

One way to do this is to come up with an affirmation that works for you. In the beginning I used the words "No one deserves to be talked to the way I am talking to myself," "You don't deserve that" and "This is not about you, you haven't done anything to deserve that" (the attack I am unloading on myself). About a year ago, Dr. Gary Berman gave me a particularly helpful affirmation, "I like myself, I love myself, and I am responsible for my present and my future." I found this affirmation to move me powerfully out of the reactive self-recriminations and empower me to own my ability to change my situation.

Self-Empathy

When we have a lifetime history of self-loathing or self-criticism, it is not easy to imagine how we can change that pattern of thinking, feeling and behaving toward ourselves. In my own experience, the only way that I could begin to achieve Self-Empathy was to see my child and adult selves differently. The reason for this is that we tend to judge our selves based on adult standards. We think that we could have or should have known as children what we know now! We think that we had options to say or do something different, which would change the situation's outcome. However, when we were children, those options were not open to us. Now that we are adults we have options that were not available to us as children. Most of the time the idea that we could have done something is based on a fantasy that we had more control than we really did.

To separate my adult self from my child self, I started to imagine myself as a child. This is not always easy, as many of us were never really allowed to be children. Nevertheless, we were all physically children once. I started by looking at photos of my children at the age at which I started despising myself. I realized then that no child deserves to be treated the way I was treating my own little self. After all, no child is responsible for the behavior of the adults around them (and neither is any adult!). Then, I started talking to my little self in nurturing, Compassionate phrases that I knew I would say to a child who thought such horrible things of themselves. I'd say things like, "Sweetie, it wasn't your fault" and "Oh, dear one, the adults were responsible, not you!"

Self-Respect

If we do not think highly of ourselves, it is impossible to have Compassion for ourselves. It is difficult to place value on anything about ourselves. How can we Respect someone so shameful? If we believe these things about ourselves, at any level, we do not think we deserve Respect from others and therefore cannot Respect ourselves.

We are no different from any other child born on the planet. We all start out as perfect little bundles of joy. None of us deserves to be treated with disRespect or have our boundaries violated. When our boundaries were violated, the only way we could make sense of it as children was to blame ourselves. We had to believe our parents, the people taking care of us, were okay. If we recognized that our parents were out of control or behaving despicably, we would have been too frightened. Therefore, we continued to believe we were to blame. But the truth is that it was not our fault.

We must learn to visualize our little, inner-self as delightful and precious, remembering that all children are born innocent. This visualization can be difficult as well. Does any baby, toddler or child deserve to be pushed aside, ignored and harmed? Do other children born into abuse deserve their fate? Of course, we can easily recognize that others did not deserve to be abused or neglected. However, we do not easily recognize the abuse when it comes to our self. Were you the only child in the universe that deserved to be treated disRespectfully? What helped me was when I realized how arrogant I was being to believe that I was the ONE child in the world who deserved that treatment or lack of Respect. This thought was so ridiculous that I had to recognize the thought as illogical.

My Story

During my first month of working at a residential treatment center for adolescents, I was anxious and excited, not just about the job, but about the people I was getting to know. One of the women working there, as the receptionist, was an older woman named Jeanine* whom I really liked. She was funny, inviting and warm. One morning she asked all the "girls" in the office to join her for lunch so that she could tell us all about her new beau. We gathered around her desk and she told us of all the wonderful things he had done for her around her house and the romantic things he had done. Without thinking much about it I popped in with the notion that she might need to be careful because it sounded like he might be a bit codependent.

Jeannine was furious. She snapped back at me that I was completely out of place and had no business making that comment, and she hadn't asked for my advice! I was crushed.

I bit my lip and snuck quietly into the bathroom to wash my face and not show the tears that were about to burst out. I then snuck out the door and as I closed the door I felt a wave of shame and couldn't hold back the tears any more. My head was flooded with shaming self-statements about my inappropriateness, about having not been considerate of her feelings, about how awful I was as a person, etc.

The shame I felt was way out of proportion to what had happened. Part of me wanted to be angry with her for having blasted me that way for something that was an innocent observation, but I knew she had a right to her upset. And, she was right; I didn't know her well enough to say something to her about her beau. The shame radiated through my entire body, wracking me with pain. Having been in therapy at that time for a couple of years, I knew what I needed to do, though I had never been able to do it before.

I stood outside the door and closed my eyes. I started talking to the little part of me that was being so overly reactive to the situation. I said to myself "You haven't done anything that horrible. She over reacted a bit, and while you may have been out of line, you certainly don't deserve the things you are saying to yourself. You were not trying to hurt her. You made a mistake, and it's okay. No one deserves to be talked to the way you are talking to yourself." I went on like this for a few minutes until I could feel the shame lifting. My tears stopped and the pain in my chest and arms slowly dissolved. I was astonished at how this changed how I felt so dramatically.

My little self had actually listened to what I said, and it had relieved the misery. I was able in a few minutes time to take myself out of the horror of the Victim place, simply by offering myself Empathy and Respect, and owning that what I did was a mistake but not a horrible infraction deserving of punishment.

Compassion for the Drama Queens that remain

Troubled people are locked into roles they despise. They are unaware that other types of interactions are possible. The desire to escape pain drives the Cycle of Egocentrism. A commitment to work through pain opens the door for Compassion. A willingness to change, to face the pain, to walk through the terror of feeling, allows us to move into the Cycle of Compassion. Not every one is cut out for it; they may be too fragile or may simply lack the courage. Ideally, more than one family member participates, but change can occur even if only one person actively engages in the process. Breaking the cycle requires only one person to change.

Living in the Cycle of Compassion allows us to experience deeply satisfying and meaningful relationships whether the other person is aware of the Cycles or not. Conflict will exist; in fact, it may surface more frequently as we take Ownership of our own feelings. Re-framing conflict with Compassion allows each person to be separate, yet accepted as a part of the others world. Relationships functioning in the Cycle of Compassion are not static; they are constantly moving, flexing and growing. Changing from Egocentrism to Compassion changes the way we interact with ourselves and with every person that we meet. From a position of strong confidence, Respect, love, Empathy, trust and Ownership we are empowered to help others achieve joy.

By choosing to respond differently than our emotions dictate, we can change the quality of our relationship with others and ourselves. By learning to respond to perceived threat with Ownership, we can learn to see our part in problems without taking possession of responsibility for other's behaviors. This results in our having Respect for how others live and the choices they make and prevents us from crossing boundaries and doing things for others that they could and should do for themselves. The result is our deepening Empathy for others and ourselves. The result is having meaningful, emotionally intimate connections with others, and a deep Respect and love for ourselves absent the shame that has bound us from connections with others and ourselves.

When we learn to listen from a place of Ownership, Empathy, and Respect, we begin to hear another person's reactivity. We have a boundary, and we know that their emotional reactions are "about them." Remember, we do not own what is not ours. Through Ownership, we empathically listen for the feelings of others with the knowledge that we do not have to "fix" anything. We Respect their experience. We understand that they must work through this experience without our help. For me, this process is something that I have to do slowly much of the time. It is rarely automatic.

Ownership, the Antidote to Being a Victim

The core of practicing Compassion is Ownership. With Ownership we are able to hold on to responsibility for our stuff, our feelings, and our needs without expecting others to do it for us, or taking over that which belongs to others. As Byron Katie says, there are four kinds of "Stuff:" God's stuff, the government's stuff, other people's stuff, and our stuff.[10] The only thing we can own is our stuff. This means, when we have a feeling reaction to something someone has said or done, we own that our reaction is about our own needs, experiences and beliefs, not about the other person. I am not ignoring cause and effect here, I am saying that the responsibility for what we feel and how we react to those feelings; belongs to us. This also means we are not responsible for the other person's feelings or reactions to what we say or do.

If you are feeling ashamed and fearful, you are in the Victim position. Of course, other feelings are also associated with the Victim. There is despair, hopelessness, helplessness, trapped, and suicidal. These are not healthy feelings. If we are trapped by those feelings, we need to find a way out as soon as possible. Returning to the old Self-Protective or Rescuing behaviors is one way to go. That is, if you want to stay miserable with no hope of getting out.

The way out that will lead to a Compassionate life is to move into Ownership. No matter what else is going on, Ownership is always a choice. Ownership is not a feeling; it is a behavior, an action. Ownership is changing how you think about and respond to a situation. Ownership is knowing that you can make a difference in how you experience what is happening. You can own your experience by communicating, taking an action or changing how you think about the situation.

The key to taking Ownership is making the choice. We have to realize that we are not our thoughts. When we get triggered into our automatic response, we can stop and make a choice to practice Ownership, Empathy or Respect.

When someone attacks you verbally, the familiar is to feel blamed and shamed. Take a moment to go to a mindful place. Notice what you are feeling. If you are immediately feeling at fault, bad about yourself, shamed, afraid of what is going to happen, but trapped in your ability to do anything about it, you are in the Victim role.

When another person is communicating with you, try to find something in what is being said that you can own. This does not mean agreeing with them that you have done something wrong. It is merely accepting that something you did caused a reaction in them.

Respect, the Antidote to Being a Rescuer

When you notice that you are feeling angry and ashamed, you are squarely in the Rescuer position. In the Rescuer position, you also feel the need to control the situation. You feel that you have the power to "fix" it, if everyone would just do what you want him or her to do or listen to what you have to say. As Rescuers, we are good at what we do. We are experts at giving good advice that makes practical sense. We feel we have a responsibility to make sure that others listen to our good advice. We want to make sure that the others know what they "should" and "should not" do. Most of the time, we feel guilty if we do not physically do what we perceive needs to be done. As a Rescuer, we feel we are "bad" if we do not do it ourselves

The antidote to rescuing is Respect. Respect others' ability to figure out what needs to be done. We only answer a question asked directly of us. We Respect that if a person wants our advice, they will ask. We do not offer unsolicited assistance. Often it is not clear what others can or cannot do for themselves. A "good" Victim works really hard to convince you that he or she is unable to do much of anything. Therefore, we have to be in our bodies. While in our bodies we will identify on a feeling level if our boundaries are being crossed. We also do not do something for someone else that is not in our best interest. We will not do something for others that cost us more than we are willing to invest. To do so would be disRespectful of ourselves! And, we can only take Ownership of things that belong to us.

This is particularly hard to do with our kids. I remember when my twins were in elementary school they were always forgetting something. They got to school about an hour before I had to leave for work, so they knew they could call me and I could bring it to them. Now, when they were in elementary school, I tended to let them get away with this. But when they hit Junior High School, I knew it was time they grew up and took care of business themselves. The first couple of months, okay, to be honest the whole first year of seventh grade, they continued to call me, even when they knew the answer. They thought I was being so mean. After all, I could drop it off on my way to work as I had done before. Why was I being this way now? They would beg and plead and explain how important this particular item was for their grades. They could get me on that one because they knew I wanted them to make good grades. But I didn't let up. Eventually they gave up. But their unhappiness was at times palpable. You see? I wasn't responsible for their being unhappy with my decision to stop enabling them.

The trick is that we tend to take on a sense of shame and badness when we feel that we could be helping someone. That's the Rescuer in us. We would rather disRespect them, by doing something for them that they can or should do for themselves than to feel the shame and guilt that comes up when we stop doing it.

Empathy, the Antidote to Being a Self-Protector

Empathy allows us to not shame ourselves for having the feelings. We give ourselves the right to have the feelings we have, to understand that we are human and of course we have feelings. We don't have to try to stop them with… well, whatever form we prefer to use to do that… We then apply the same thing to others. We allow them to have their feelings, knowing that as humans we have feelings for a reason, even if they are not completely evident at the moment.

Fear and anger swell up inside us when we are in the Self-Protector position. Often when we feel we are attacked, we react as a Self-Protector. We don't think we have any choice but to attack or withdraw into a protective barrier in order to be safe. We don't want to lose our dignity and fall into the Victim position. We might not be aware of the feeling of fear, but it's there. As Self-Protectors, we block fear. Fear makes us feel small and powerless. We puff up and try to show those around us that we are not little and vulnerable. We want others to know that we have rights. We want others to know that we are being treated poorly.

When we are in the Self-Protector mode the other person's needs and feelings are not part of the equation. All we can be present for is our sense of being wronged or wounded. Moving into Empathy when all of out attention is on our own wounds feels counter-intuitive to us.

This is the real test of our ability to practice Compassion. Of course it's virtually impossible to always be able to do it. It can be terrifying to let down our protective barriers long enough to let into another's pain. At the time it is happening it doesn't even feel like it makes sense. But it is how Compassion is won.

When we take a moment to re-focus our attention on the other person, we find out what is really taking place. That can be scary and make us feel more vulnerable. At that moment, it can feel very threatening.

Deepening Your Work

If you are one of the few people who want to free yourself entirely from the Cycle of Egocentrism then you will want to take your work to the next level. You will find the **Oh, WOW This changes everything! DVD & Workbook** is your guide through the process. The DVD & Workbook clearly direct you through the process making it easier and easier to make the shift. You can get them now at: www.ohwowthischangeseverything.com

Chapter Take Aways

√ Becoming Compassionate starts with accepting that we are all basically the same and that our automatic responses can be changed.

√ Our instinctive emotional responses are compelling and often irresistible.

√ Developing this Innter Witness aspect of ourselves teaches us that who we are, the essence our self, is separate from what we experience in our lives.

√ Compassion must include self-love.

√ Come up with an affirmation that works for you to reduce shame.

√ A commitment to work through pain opens the door for Compassion.

√ Ownership is verbalizing that we recognize what is going on inside of us.

√ Ownership is the Antidote to Being a Victim.

√ Respect is the Antidote to Being a Rescuer.

√ Empathy is the Antidote to Being a Self-Protector.

CHAPTER 7

When the Shift Happens

Empowered Communication

Standing in front of her out of control class of 5th graders, my grandmother used to start whispering her commands to the kids. The class would start to settle down as each child, one by one, got curious about what it was she was telling them. This was her way of empowering herself to regain control of the situation. My grandmother had a great sense of personal control, which is what drew her students to listen to her. Contrast that to the urban school that my daughters were subjected to for a few weeks. Every time I walked into the school I could hear a cacophony of voices yelling at different pitches coming from every classroom. The teachers more mature voices could be heard above them all. It was clear that yelling was the only tool they had in their toolbox to manage their classroom. Their attempts at moving into louder and louder Self-Protector behavior seemed to only escalate the classrooms.

Empowered communication is adding tools to your toolbox and information into your decision making process that will give you more options as to how to manage your relationships and your life.

Attending to our Reactions

Breathe before I react

Breathing may seem simple, but it is not. Our bodies react to the sense of being attacked by reflexively going into a highly aroused state. In this state our breathing can stop, our heartbeat speeds up and our muscles tighten. When we are under attack (or feel like we are) our adrenal glands kicks into gear, loading us up with the fight or flight hormone adrenaline. The best way to reduce the rush of adrenaline is to relax and take slow, deep breaths.

Remember the real person who is talking

At the moment we feel that we are being attacked, we unconsciously react to our "perception" of the person in front of us. Some part of our brain sees them as someone from our past: someone from our past who may have hurt us, someone who hurt us deliberately. At this point we have a choice stay in the Cycle of

Egocentrism (which our body is telling us is what we have to do) or we can stop and consider what we know about the person in front of us.

Remembering what we know about this person's history with us and feelings for us helps us be less reactive. If we contain our primitive reaction, we can own our part in what they are saying. We can see that it is not all about us. It is also about their hurt and their history. Knowing this, we can accept our part and feel Empathy for them.

Okay, but what to I do?

Now we have to take an action. We have to actively do something that moves us into the practice of Compassion. It isn't easy. It's emotionally and strategically difficult, and sometimes, overwhelming, to do. We have to communicate differently; we have to think about others and ourselves differently. Here's how:

Learn Containment:

Pay attention to what is happening in your body, what you are feeling? Then hold back your responses long enough to really listen to what is being said. Our reactivity has more to do with our own history and expectations than it does with what the other person has said or done. This does not mean not to feel it! It just means you wait to express what is going on with you until you have heard the other person out. Containment is keeping your reactions to their communication to yourself until you have heard what they have to say.[11]

Listen actively:

Rather than react to any situation that comes our way, we can stop and listen to what is being said verbally and non-verbally. This communicates Respect for the other person and it conveys that you care enough to listen to their perspective. Attend to what is going on emotionally by making statements like, "Wow, I can see this really upset you."

Mirror:

As we become observers of others and ourselves we can begin to comment on what we see without judgment by "mirroring" what is happening.[11] Mirroring is observing what is being communicated and stating it back without judging or reframing it. Example: "I can see that your feelings are hurt" or "You are saying that I have hurt your feelings"

Validate:

After the other person has had a chance to fully say what they want to say to us, we can let them know that it makes sense that they could feel the way they do, given the way they perceive things. With validation we take what we know about the other person and let them know that we understand where they are coming from.[1] This is how we communicate Respect. It's really important to understand that validation is not agreement, it is simply, saying that we understand how they could feel the way they do given how they perceive the situation. Example: "I can understand how you could feel hurt since you thought that I was angry because of you" or "It makes sense that you would feel afraid of my anger since your father used to hit you when he was angry."

Empathize:

When we Empathize with someone we use our own experience to relate to them and how they feel in this circumstance. To Empathize we take a piece of our own history and connect it with how the person is saying that they feel in this moment. [11] Example: "I felt hurt when my mom used to say things like that to me, too."

Take Ownership:

Verbalize that we recognize what is going on inside of us. By being honest with ourselves and with the other person about what is really going on inside of us, we open ourselves to participate fully in the relationship. Example: "I noticed that I did have the thought that you were not doing it right. I got scared that our plans wouldn't work the way I wanted them to work."

Internalize the process

This works inside of us as well as outside. When we find ourselves in situations that do not involve others, or where, for whatever reason, we can't communicate with the other person, we have no choice but to take this process inside. By listening to what we are really feeling, validating our right to feel the way that we do, experiencing Empathy for the parts of us that feel what we feel and then taking Ownership for what we feel and how we react, we can respond to ourselves from an empowered position.

Chris' and Stanley's Story

Chris* was a cute, petite tennis instructor at a very elite tennis club. Stanley*, Chris's husband of 21 years, was a successful Architect and had just made partner. Chris and Stanley had three beautiful, athletic kids who all played tennis and took lessons at the club where Chris worked. Stanley was being called away for work more and more, now that he made partner. Chris's mother had been a neglectful alcoholic and had not been in Chris's life for a long time, but her father had been the guiding light in Chris's painful childhood. This continued to be true as he had moved into their neighborhood and helped Chris with the kids since Stanley made partner. Without warning, Chris's father died of a heart attack in his sleep. Chris went into a deep depression and struggled to find her way out. She got a face lift and went to a psychiatrist who put her on anti-depressants. Nothing seemed to help. Fortunately, her kids' tennis instructor, whom Chris worked with every day, filled the void. Chris talked to him several times a day and had lunch with him most days. They went to tournaments together and often stayed after work for drinks in the bar at the club. Stanley was gone so much that he really didn't notice, at first. Stanley began to notice that Chris was coming home later and later from work and that she often appeared giddy and school-girlish. Stanley became quite possessive, demanding that Chris call him at appointed times and insisting that he should know where she was at all times. Finally Stanley confronted her when he found her at the bar late after work, drinking with him. Chris admitted that she had slept with him, once and that she now knows it was a mistake.

Stanley's sense of betrayal was deep. He had always trusted Chris completely, never questioning her loyalty or her love of him. Now he was devastated and thrown into complete terror of her every move. He berated her for her betrayal and verbally abused her on a daily basis. His anger was all encompassing and took over their relationship.

Chris was just as devastated. She had no clue as to why she fell into the relationship with her children's tennis instructor. After confessing to Stanley, she immediately broke it off with the tennis instructor and pled with Stanley for his forgiveness. Her depression returned and she thought of suicide, even toying with a gun that they had hidden in a safe. Stanley was so angry with her that he took it out, loaded it and placed it on the counter and told her to use it.

By the time they came in to therapy they were not sure they were going to make it as a couple. They had discussed divorce and were at a loss as to how to proceed. But in spite of everything that had happened, Stanley admitted that he still loved Chris and that he wanted nothing more than to have their relationship back as it had been before. Chris, too, felt that there had been nothing wrong with the relationship except for her infidelity and that if Stanley could forgive her, she just wanted things back as they had been.

In therapy we worked on understanding the roles that they now found themselves in and how they had gotten themselves there. Then, they learned how to communicate Compassionately as a step in overcoming the shame, pain and anger that then dictated their every interaction.

Chris was squarely in the Victim position. To get herself out she would have to take Ownership of what she had done without falling further into the Victim pit. When someone has done something as egregious as having an affair, it's difficult to find the self-Empathy required to avoid falling into beating themselves up with negative self-statements and becoming their own perpetrator. In order to do this, she would have to take some Ownership of the condition the marriage was in prior to her affair, and Respect him enough to say how it was for her.

Stanley had to find a way to have Empathy for someone who had hurt him as deeply as anyone could hurt him. In order to do this, he had to take Ownership of his part in contributing to the state of their relationship prior to the affair. He would have to move out of the blame game and into Ownership. He would have to see himself as an active participant in the relationship, including its disasters (i.e. the affair) and take an honest account of how he contributed to the affair happening, without taking the blame.

The moment the paradigm shift occurred was during a conversation in therapy in which they both began to take Ownership and allow each other Empathy.

Stanley demanded, "How could you do this? I can't leave you and I can't stay. I am so hurt that I cry all the time now. I never used to cry."

In tears, Chris told Stanley, "I know, I know, I am so sorry I did this to us. But you know, I was so lonely. You were gone all the time and, well, after my Dad died I just felt so lost."

Stanley began to well up with tears, which he held back. "I'm sorry Chris. I never thought about how hard that must have been. I'm a terrible husband."

"No," Chris said, "You're not. I should have told you how I was feeling."

"I should have noticed. But I was so busy with work, I never saw what you were going through." He put his arms around her and they cried together, for a long time.

The story wasn't over there; they still had lots of work to do. But the crisis was over. They had both Owned their part of the problem and expressed Empathy for what the other was feeling and maintained a sense of Respect for themselves, and for the other.

Chapter Take Aways

- ✓ Breathe before you react.

- ✓ Containment is keeping your reactions to their communication to yourself until you have heard what the other person has to say.

- ✓ Rather than react to any situation that comes our way, we can stop and listen to what is being said verbally and non-verbally.

- ✓ Mirroring is observing what is being communicated and stating it back without judging or reframing it.

- ✓ Validation is not agreement, it is simply, saying that we understand how they could feel the way they do given how they perceive the situation.

- ✓ To empathize we take a piece of our own history and connect it with how the person is saying that they feel in this moment.

CHAPTER 8

Driving in a Different Gear

A whole new map

Lisa* pushed the CD into the player and a slow, sweet waltz began to play. She had pushed all the furniture in the dining room back so that the hardwood floor was exposed. Danny stuck his head in from his office and told her he'd be right there. A few moments later Danny came in and swept Lisa in his arms as they waltzed around the dining room together. Just months before Lisa had been in my office chagrined and unhappy, sure that she and Danny were on the verge of a divorce.

Wayne* and his 17-year-old son James worked all day together on one of James' last badges for him to complete his Eagle Scout honors. At the end of the day they plunged into their pool and roughhoused for about an hour. After their swim they picked up James' girlfriend and went to see a movie. Two months before Wayne had been nagging James about completing his schoolwork, chores and badge work. James had become so resentful of his father that he was refusing to do anything his dad asked of him and had become belligerent when Wayne tried to talk to him about anything. James was becoming depressed and withdrawing from his activities.

Life can be easier, more fun and less conflictual when we learn Compassion. Our relationships take on a new level of connectivity and meaning. We like others and ourselves better.

Our relationship with ourselves

Our battle with Egocentrism starts with how we see ourselves. The biggest challenge is overcoming our own belief that we are to "blame" for whatever happens in our life (talk about Egocentrism!).

When we heal our own shame and blame, then we are much more likely to be able to see others with Compassion. It's odd, in a way, to think that how we think of ourselves changes how we think of others, but it's so true. Once Oprah interviewed some men from a prison who were sentenced either to death or to a life sentence for murder. They talked about how they had seen themselves as not worth anything, and not mattering to anyone. This belief turned into an attitude of complete disregard for anyone or anything. Their own life was meaningless and therefore, to them, no one else's life had any meaning either. Their complete disregard for life came from their own shame and self-loathing; a typical Victim position turned into Self-Protector and then, ultimately, into the worst kind of predator.

The truth is that all of us are precious gifts to the world, even those of us who are not so perfect (who is?). Those of us who have made mistakes (who hasn't) and those of us who have done outright horrid things (who of us hasn't done things we are not proud of?) are all at core precious gifts, who are doing the best we can with the attitudes and beliefs that we have.

Compassionate Relationships

Practicing the things we have learned about the Cycle of Compassion in our relationships creates the beginnings of healthy relationships. Having Empathy can be a scary process. Empathy will bring us into deeper, more trusting connection with others and ourselves. Practicing Ownership empowers us to step out, take risks, and become who we are meant to be. Ownership will allow us to see others for whom they are really. Learning to Respect others and ourselves builds deep pride in our relationships as well as ourselves.

Conflict still happens, of course; in fact, it may surface more frequently as we take Ownership of our own feelings. Re-framing conflict with Compassion allows each person to be separate, yet accepted as a part of the others world. Relationships functioning in the Cycle of Compassion are not static; they are constantly moving, flexing and growing. Changing from Egocentrism to Compassion changes the way we interact with ourselves and with every person that we meet. From a position of strong confidence, Respect, love, Empathy, trust and Ownership we are empowered to help others achieve joy.

Recently a couple I was working with got caught in a conflict that they didn't see coming. Joan* simply asked Jonathan* if he had asked his daughter about what gift to get their grandson. It was a simple trigger where Jonathan felt he had "screwed up" by not remembering to do something Joan had asked him to do. But rather than reacting defensively, as was his pattern, he stopped, took a breath and said, "I'm sorry. It slipped my mind because we were talking about the car (she was buying from them). I'll call her right now." Joan never even knew that Jonathan had been triggered, until he said, "I feel really ashamed that I let you down." That gave Joan an opportunity to show him Empathy and thank him for his choice to do things differently.

Joan said, "I know there has been a lot going on this week with Donna (their daughter) and I really appreciate that while you didn't remember to call, you did remember that it was important to me."

To practice Compassion in our relationships is one of the greatest challenges of living in the Cycle of Compassion. Tolerating relationships with those who do not listen to us or abuse us in some way is not practicing self-care. Yet, many of our relationships may have qualities that we enjoy even when the relationship is at times hurtful. We have to create a path that will allow us to both care for ourselves and to not blame and judge those we love.

Our relationships are, by definition, ours. We own responsibility for the quality and progression of the connections we establish. By practicing stewardship, we own our behaviors, actions,and words. We do not take on responsibility for the emotions and reactions of others. We are aware that our own needs are our own responsibility. However, meeting our needs does not come at the expense of another person. We then communicate to the other person that their needs are important to us as well.

Relationships at Home

Home is where the Cycle of Egocentrism originates, in our family of origin. If the original wounding that drives the Cycle is not grieved and processed, the Cycle continues throughout our life times until the grief is worked through.

How this plays out at home is that whatever primary ego identification we chose for ourselves continues to be played out in our current relationships. The feelings, drives and beliefs that we accepted as truth as a child will continue to create the same plot, again and again. The patterns of interactions that we experienced as so tremendously painful as a child, will haunt us through or closest and most needed intimate relationships.

We can make different choices, even with those people that hold the greatest triggers for us. A client of mine is moving in with her mother, after having been on her own for about ten years. My client, Karen*, is 30 years old and worked very hard to overcome the severe neglect from her mother and abuse by her father. Karen just completed her MBA and got her first job, but with a slew of student loans, she will need some financial relief while she begins her career. Her mother needed help with her house payment, too since her husband had just passed. Karen came to me with her stress about how triggered she is by her mother's behavior, which is unchanged since Karen's childhood. Karen began to open her heart to understand the pain her mother felt married to an abusive husband and having been raised by fundamentalist parents. Karen realized that her mother's indifference toward her was not about her, but about her mothers' need to remain distant and in her Self-Protective stance in order to feel safe. At that point, Karen was able to move in with her mother, and accept her mother for who she is without taking her mothers' behavior toward her personally.

She transformed her relationship with her mother by transforming how she thought about her mother and developing Empathy for what her mother has been through.

Relationships at Work

Jennifer* was fuming as she listened to her voice mail. Her gut reaction to her boss's demand that she work overtime, again, when she had just finished a 80 hour week to help finish a rush project, was that he was just a real "jerk." But before she reacted she sat in her cubicle and breathed. She took her time before calling him back and responding, she wanted to be sure that she was coming from a place of Compassion rather than from the defensiveness her natural impulses would have her react. She closed her eyes and went into that mindful place as she thought things through. Her boss had been on vacation last week and didn't know that she had just come off an 80-hour week. He just knew that the project had finished on time and while he was happy about that, he was anxious about the new client that had just come on board, who had a history of having just been burned by an unethical accounting company. Actually, as she thought about it mindfully, she realized that he had asked her to help him with this because he felt she was the person he most wanted at his side to handle this difficult situation. It had been a compliment and she had been about to respond to it as though she had been attacked. It didn't change that she was exhausted and couldn't really do what he was asking her, but it did change how she responded. When Jennifer called him she was open, and empathetic. She told him that she appreciated his wanting her in on this project and then explained to him that she had just come off an exhausting week and asked if there was some other way she could help him this week. While he was disappointed, he was able to hear her and made alternate plans.

Many opportunities exist because the competitive and structural components of employment often replicate the drama of the Cycle of Egocentrism. Responding with Compassion requires vigilance and determination to "be the change we want to see in the world" (Mahatma Ghandi).

Potential Victims will conclude that our boss or company

is taking advantage of us, and feel that we are not valued because we are tired or overworked. Instead, we can either change jobs, or talk to our supervisor about what we need. We take Ownership of the situation and recognize that what is happening in our work environment is not really all about us. We ask for help when we need it, too.

Potential Rescuers attempt to take care of every detail of everyone's job, over-extending our self and then feeling resentful that no one seems to be appreciative. Letting go of our need to take care of everyone else we can start noticing that others are doing things in the ways that work for them. We stop trying to save them from themselves, but trust them to take care of what they need to for themselves. This doesn't mean not being helpful, it just means not doing for others what they can and should do for themselves.

Potential Self-Protectors find ourselves having to defend everything we do and feeling fearful of someone undermining our authority or "ratting" on us to the boss. Instead we risk being open with someone we trust about what we need and what we are worried about. We choose to see others as also trying to get what they need and being afraid as well. In Compassion we soften our defenses and notice where others could be willing to help us if we ask them.

Our Relationships with Friends

My friend Charlotte* is a supreme Self-Protector. She came from a family in which her mother was a raging alcoholic and her father was an aggressive, sexual perpetrator. Charlotte is loving and thoughtful, but she struggles with seeing everything as an attack and fearing that she is never getting fair treatment. When we first met my life was a mess. I was as single mom and struggling financially, I was in need of a lot of support and fell into the Victim role with most of my friendships. Most of my friends were primarily Rescuers and we had a regular Cycle of Egocentrism playing out during those early years. Charlotte was willing to tolerate me as long as I was in the Victim position, since that position didn't really threaten her. But as I grew stronger and worked to move myself out of the Victim position, Charlotte didn't know where to put me. Once I moved into a place were I didn't seem to need anyone to take care of me, I was no longer in the Victim role and therefore I must be a Self-Protector. That didn't feel safe to her. I continued to include her in my social events and invited her to lunches, and she came, but clearly felt uncomfortable. Eventually she stopped returning my calls and dropped out of my life. It was painful for me, but I understood that her inability to shift me into a different role was not about me, but about her and where she is in her life.

Our primary ego identifications (or role in the Cycle of Egocentrism) do not escape being played out in each and every one of our relationships, including our friendships.

We will find people we can rescue and people that we end up having to feel defensive against. We will be hurt and Victimized in the same way by these friends as we were by our original relationships. In the Cycle we keep our relationships distant (Self-Protectors and Rescuers) and refuse to let ourselves feel vulnerable (fear or shame) in order to avoid the grief. Still others of us find ourselves being confused by how people use us and take advantage of us (Victims). This dynamic results in our finding many creative ways to use people for a false sense of connectedness in order to maintain an illusion of friendship.

Still another sad dynamic is those of us that are so afraid of real intimacy that we will perceive anyone we come into conflict with as being a Self-Protector and we percieve ourselves to be the Victim We then immediately cut ourselves off from them either emotionally or physically. This results in the abandonment of connection through Self-Protective measures that puts the perceived perpetrator in the Victim position.

Once we move into Compassion we come from a place that acknowledges that we have value, and that the other has value. We judge everyone we meet as doing the best they can with what the resources they have available to them. When we are in the Cycle of Compassion we let ourselves be aware of those that are dangerous to us. Yet we keep ourselves safe without going into a defensive posture that communicates we consider the other to be a bad person.

We allow ourselves to have our feelings and communicate them to those we experience as available to hear them. We Respect other people's abilities and don't jump in to do things for others that they can and should do for themselves. Our relationships are reciprocal; we can ask for help as well as give help when appropriate.

A World Without Drama

Our Egocentric World

Here in the United States, we have become the worlds Rescuer. On the worldwide political stage we are continually turned to for the Rescuing of third world countries, of oppressed peoples and natural disasters. This is how America is playing out the Cycle of Egocentrism in the world arena. The events of September 11, 2001 resulted, for the first time, in the United States being viewed as a Victim. The world resoundingly responded with words of support and encouragement, yet since there are no other Rescuers available, as a nation, we began to act as Self-Protectors. The Alqueda became the target for our blame and rage, and Afghanistan the setting for the drama. Next Americans find themselves engaged in the Cycle of Egocentrism as the Self-Protector against the dictator of Iraq and as Rescuers (of the Iraqi people). Both roles engender hatred by the rest of the players. Rescuers anger those that we think we are rescuing because the Rescuer always thinks we know how things should be. Self-Protectors anger everyone because we are perceived of as being perpetrators of abuse of power. Americans can only hope to disengage from the triangle through displaying vast amount of true Compassion at the end of the military action. It will not work for America or the United Nations to continue the Cycle of Egocentrism through continuing in the Rescuer position. To do so will continue to anger and disable the Iraqi people, preventing them from moving out of the Cycle of Egocentrism themselves and leaving them stuck interminably in the Victim position.

"We are All Doing the Best We Can!"

When in the Cycle of Compassion we respond to our own, and other people's pain with Empathy and Respect. We own our part in it and honor the other persons' part in their own pain. We allow ourselves, and others, to be imperfect, and trust that we, and they, will keep doing the best we can.

We can expect that it will not be an easy process. We well forget to be Compassionate with ourselves. We will forget to take care of something important to us. We will step on someone else's toes and not take Ownership for it. Sometimes the pain, anger and fear awakened in the Wall of Grief will feel overwhelming. We will fall into the Victim hole and not realize it. That is all to be expected in the process.

But stress is remarkably reduced when we are no longer struggling under the assumption that people are either out to get us or are there just to help us. The worry that is saved by the simple assumption that "we are all doing the best we can" is immense. It alters how we think of ourselves, our families of origin, our current family, our co-workers, even the politicians we listen to on TV. Instead of being angry all the time for what they could have or should have been doing, we can accept that they have done the best they could.

This does not mean that we don't speak up for injustice. It is our part of the bargain that we take Ownership of the things in our lives, even in our world, that are not right and do what we can to change them. But we no longer condemn those who allow such things to happen, we try to make things be different for all of us. We stop judging others and ourselves as being "bad" because we failed to do things that needed to be done. We own what we did or didn't do, and we forgive ourselves for not being perfect. We accept our limitations while doing our best to make it be different in the future.

Living life in the Cycle of Compassion is a process. Our innate survival instincts will resist any new process. Therefore, we will struggle daily between the old way of being and our new choice of Compassion. Once we have moved into the Cycle of Compassion, we will glimpse the possible joy here for us. When we experience this joy, it is impossible not to want more. The love, connection and joy will help us get through the rough times. Within the Cycle, we know that life can be drama free. We can change our thoughts and move out of misery and into joyfulness. That doesn't mean it's easy.

Congratulations!

Now that you have completed this book you have a chance to live your life with Compassion and joy. I am excited for you. I know it's hard work, but believe me, you are worth it!

Remember, f you are one of the few people who want to free yourself entirely from the Cycle of Egocentrism then you will want to take your work to the next level. You will find the **Oh, WOW This changes everything! DVD & Workbook** is your guide through

Melody Brooke, Author

After a childhood of abuse and neglect and two failed marriages Melody decided there had to be a better way. Counselors and self-help books agreed that it was her parent's and husband's fault. Applying this new knowledge widened the gulf between them. It didn't take much of this before she KNEW there had to be a better way. With three kids to take care of, she needed to find it fast. Well, it took a dozen years to grasp how alike we really are, and more importantly, how to bridge the gap between us when all seems lost.

Melody first worked with adolescents and their families. Success required helping everyone see each other's perspective. When Melody entered private practice she was drawn to working with severely emotionally disturbed clients. Behind their seemingly irrational behavior she saw rational processes controlled by a viewpoint distorted by years of abuse Melody's model evolved from understanding the distortions her clients used to survive in a scary world. Her techniques transformed their lives and allowed many of them to return to the workplace for the first time in decades. The results are just as remarkable when applied to couples, families, and even in the workplace. What she loves about sharing these tools with "normal" people is the ripple effect it has on their children, spouses, parents, and co-workers.

Practicing what she preaches, Melody is now happily married and has five children enjoying the ripple effect in her life.

Melody is a Professional Counselor and Marriage and Family Therapist, graduating Texas Woman's University in 1989. She is published in Radix Journal, Dallas Recovery Magazine, The Southwest Morticians Journal, Plano Child Magazine, and on the Dan and Jennifer Relationship website.

I'd love to hear your comments and questions.
Please send me an email me at:
melody@ohwowthischangeseverything.com

See how the cycles work everywhere from the world stage to the bedroom, visit my blog at: ohwowthischangeseverything.com/blog

Also by Melody Brooke:

The Cycles of the Heart: A way out of the Egocentrism of everyday life

Available online at: www.melodybrooke.com

Melody helps people and businesses who want happiness and success to develop a collaborative culture in their lives and work.

Book Melody to present practical applications of the cycles at your event:

www.ohwowthischangeseverything.com

NOTES

These pages are for you to save the most useful ideas you found in this book or, even better, your own "Oh Wow" moments.

I'd love for you to share them with me by email at melody@ohwowthischangeseverything.com

Made in the USA